Expert Mediators

Expert Mediators

Overcoming Mediation Challenges in Workplace, Family, and Community Conflicts

Jean Poitras, PhD
and
Susan Raines, PhD

JASON ARONSON
Lanham • Boulder • New York • Toronto • Plymouth, UK

Published by Jason Aronson
A wholly owned subsidiary of The Rowman & Littlefield Publishing Group, Inc.
4501 Forbes Boulevard, Suite 200, Lanham, Maryland 20706
www.rowman.com

10 Thornbury Road, Plymouth PL6 7PP, United Kingdom

British Library Cataloguing in Publication Information Available

Library of Congress Cataloging-in-Publication Data

Poitras, Jean, 1968-
Expert mediators overcoming mediation challenges in workplace, family, and community conflicts / Jean Poitras and Susan Raines.
p. cm.
Includes bibliographical references and index.
ISBN 978-0-7657-0963-9 (cloth : alk. paper) -- ISBN 978-0-7657-0964-6 (electronic)
1. Mediation. 2. Mediators (Persons)--Legal status, laws, etc. 3. Dispute resolution (Law) 4. Conflict management. I. Raines, Susan. II. Title.
K2390.P65 2013
303.6'9--dc23
2012031938

™ The paper used in this publication meets the minimum requirements of American National Standard for Information Sciences Permanence of Paper for Printed Library Materials, ANSI/NISO Z39.48-1992.

Printed in the United States of America

Contents

Acknowledgments

Thank you to all the mediators who so generously shared their experience and wisdom and made this book possible.

The writing of this book was supported, in part, by funding from a grant to assist with the publication and dissemination of research from HEC Montréal (Canada) and a grant from the Dean of Humanities and Social Sciences at Kennesaw State University (United States).

Introduction

What is Needed to Move Mediation Expertise Forward?

I left the mediation training feeling well prepared to start my career as a mediator. I read many mediation books. We practiced our opening statements, role-played, discussed ethical dilemmas, and examined ways to overcome impasses. Then, when I tried to mediate my first case, I was caught like a deer in headlights—uncertain which technique to try and I felt lost when the parties seemed stuck in their positions. After barely an hour I declared an impasse. I loved my mediation training experience, but in reality, it did not give me enough guidance to know how to deal with specific problems that were likely to arise in real mediations. How do I develop that knowledge base without making my clients pay the price as I develop my skills through trial and error?

Whether you have been mediating fifteen years or fifteen minutes, every mediator gets stumped from time to time and wishes he could brainstorm process options with other mediators. Yet, most neutrals complete their cases and seldom get the opportunity to debrief or share ideas with their peers or those who have more experience.

In the three decades that mediation's use has been growing in the United States and elsewhere, much has been written about its philosophical underpinnings, its ethical dilemmas, and its application both inside and outside judicial systems. Individual practitioners or small teams of researchers have shed light on specific aspects of mediation, such as how to separate interests from positions, the importance of listening skills, and the use of different models like evaluative, facilitative, and transformative mediation. However, some very basic challenges remain: how to deal with entrenched positions, strong emotions, and cultural differences? Mediation expertise is truly achieved when a mediator learns to overcome these challenges through experience and intuition. But what if that learning curve could be reduced? For experienced mediators who wonder "how would a different mediator handle this?" we have some ideas to share.

Whatever type of mediation cases you are handling (civil, commercial, workplace, community, or family) and whatever type of mediation you are practicing (evaluative, facilitative, or transformative), there are some common, great challenges that you are likely to face. Several books have wonderfully described mediation processes and generic mediator skills. Unfortunately, these reflections do not address specific, common mediation challenges. Despite decades of publication and research, there is still a lack of research on how to overcome these challenges, as mediation books tend to focus on generic processes and skills.

FOCUSING ON THE BEST PRACTICES

Mediation is usually presented as a process that moves parties through a series of steps to get them closer and closer to resolution. Mediation steps can vary from four to more than twelve steps depending on how much detail the authors use to describe the process. Irrespective of the author, nearly all mediation processes in the West involve these elements: initiating dialogue, looking for common interests, brainstorming options, and adopting a solution. Descriptions of the mediation process are usually complemented by a presentation of generic skills that help move the process along. While the mediation steps almost always follow a generic order, the set of skills needed to help parties resolve conflicts may vary depending on mediation models.

Each model proposes a set of principles that should guide mediators' interventions. For example, the evaluative style of mediation proposes that mediators help parties assess the likelihood that their case will prevail in court. The idea is that when parties are more realistic about their case, they are more open to compromise. Facilitative or problem-solving mediation states that mediators should help parties look behind their positions to get them to identify and clarify their needs (also known as interests). The idea is that when parties focus on their interests, rather than their positions, they have more room to negotiate a compromise. Transformative mediation proposes, among other things, that mediators encourage parties to recognize each other's needs and to empower the parties to solve their own disputes. The objective is to improve relationships, which will later transform the confrontation into a search for common solutions.

However, when confronted with some basic mediation challenges, generic process skills and philosophies are inadequate. They lack the specificity needed to know how and when to apply them. How do you deal with a party who is stuck in the past? How do you deal with parties who feel they have been wronged? Too often, junior mediators are overwhelmed with the challenges they face in mediation. Their basic training has not prepared them to deal with these specific issues. However, as they become more experienced they are able to better recognize, diagnose, and apply the appropriate best practices to overcome these challenges.

What is needed to move mediation practice one step further is a collection of best practices to resolve these challenges. Mediators need to know how and when to apply specific mediation techniques. They need to learn these techniques from expert mediators, in order to shorten their learning curves. Even experienced mediators appreciate hearing the advice of their peers as they gain ideas about framing techniques and ways to address common challenges.

IDENTIFYING THE BEST PRACTICES

The best practices are generally accepted strategies that have proven themselves over time to overcome given challenges. How do we learn these best practices? Mediation practices are usually derived from two sources: a theoretic framework or an author's mediation practice. While the first avenue is usually intended as a extrapolation of how a theory would apply to a specific problem, the second one usually has a marketing twist as the author wants to demonstrate his mediation expertise and grow his reputation. Both avenues are flawed when it comes to identifying the best practices to deal with mediation challenges.

Although theory-based strategies offer great rationales about why they should work, they have not always been tested empirically to assure they actually work. A strategy may work in one context, but not in another. Experienced mediators know that one-size-fits-all strategies do not work well in conflict management. To be efficient, the best practices should be adapted to the underlying causes of the challenges in mediations.

On the other hand, strategies derived from the author's mediation practice often lack validity because they are too vulnerable to confirmation bias. Should an author believe his proposed strategy works, he will likely find plenty of evidence that the strategy does indeed work. Does one author's self-confidence in his own wisdom really guarantee success when the proposed strategies are applied by different mediators in various contexts? To be efficient, the best practices should not be mediator-specific.

What is truly needed is research based on the collective wisdom of expert mediators. Pooling expert mediators' wisdom would not only improve transferability, but would also improve the validity of the proposed best practices. How can we tap expert mediators' knowledge to overcome mediation's most frequent challenges? A powerful approach is to simply benchmark mediator best practices.

BENCHMARKING EXPERT MEDIATORS

Put simply, benchmarking is a process for identifying and implementing better or best practices. Since the goal of benchmarking is to improve mediator performance, the process seeks to identify how successful mediators overcome challenges that hinder the mediation process. It follows three basic steps: (1) the identification of mediation's greatest challenges, (2) the constitution of a pool of successful and experienced mediators, and (3) the identification of the best practices used by these mediators to overcome these challenges.

Simply identifying practices without understanding the context of their efficient use would be blind benchmarking. Selecting a practice to overcome a challenge depends on the underlying cause of the problem. Depending on the cause of a problem, the best practice to overcome it may change. Thus, identifying the best practices also requires sorting out root causes of these challenges.

Furthermore, timing is important in mediation. For example, while a reality check might be a good practice to overcome some problems, it might blow up when used too early in the process. Mediators must first build a minimum level of trust with the parties to apply a reality check strategy. Without this minimal trust level, the mediation might not be ripe enough to use reality check. Therefore, applying the best practices also requires being able to assess the risks and adopt strategies to mitigate those risks.

The goal of this book is to understand how expert mediators overcome mediation challenges. Furthermore, we will make sure we are generating high quality benchmarking results by not only identifying the best practices, but also by understanding the conditions under which each practice should be used, and the level of risk associated with the use of each strategy and technique.

LEARNING TO OVERCOME MEDIATION'S GREATEST CHALLENGES

The next chapter will describe the benchmarking process we used to identify mediation's greatest challenges and how we pooled the best practices from a large panel of expert mediators. Each of the following chapters will address one of the mediation challenges. In each process chapter, we describe the reasons why the challenge is so, well, challenging. We list and describe strategies and techniques that provide advice about how to address each challenge. Furthermore, we explore the root causes of each challenge in order to pinpoint what strategies may work best depending on the cause. We describe when to use the different techniques and the risks associated with each. Lastly, we provide examples and stories from our mediators that illustrate how and why these strategies work. Throughout the book, we provide references to other research to help guide readers toward more information on specific techniques and theories of conflict resolution.

Chapter One

Tapping Expert Mediators' Knowledge

One big threat to mediation's success is a mediation process breakdown, which is often referred to as an impasse. There is no single root cause for mediation breakdown, but rather a set of challenges, that if not resolved, may lead to an impasse. In this book, we are discovering and integrating the best practices to overcome mediation challenges, thereby improving the likelihood of settling disputes.

Although mediation challenges are numerous and may sometimes be case specific, we believe that some of the challenges are generic. This would mean that these challenges will be present on a regular basis in mediation cases, and will not be dependent on mediation contexts. Furthermore, these generic challenges should not disappear with experience; experienced mediators will still face theses challenges, but will have developed expertise to overcome them. Thus, we are referring to the challenges that are not context specific and do not disappear with experience.

The best practices are techniques or strategies used to perform steps of the mediation process. Not all practices are best practices. Only when a practice is linked to increased performance—which in this case means overcoming a challenge—does a practice become a best practice. If we assume that successful mediators overcome mediation challenges by choosing successful strategies for the challenges they face, then studying expert mediators should reveal these best practices. Therefore, we are referring to the best practices as the strategies expert mediators use to overcome challenges.

The core question of this book can be framed this way: how do expert mediators overcome mediation's greatest challenges and thus avoid mediation impasses? To answer this question, we need a pool of expert mediators, a list of mediation's greatest challenges, and a process to pinpoint and flesh out the best practices to overcome these challenges.

SAMPLING EXPERT MEDIATORS

In order to create a sample of expert mediators from a variety of practice specialties, we began by asking mediation program directors to nominate their best mediators for our study. This worked well for the court-connected mediators. For mediators working outside of the court system, such as those working as youth, elder care, environmental and public policy, and organizational mediators, we used a different strategy. First, we hand-selected mediators who have built national or international reputations based on their work. Then we asked them to recommend other experienced mediators to participate. This is called snowball sampling. A total of 186 mediators completed a survey on mediation challenges, which is a high number given the fact we were inviting only expert mediators to participate in this project. The survey was used to select expert mediators as well as to pin point the best practices.

For the benchmarking project, we wanted mediators from diverse specialties and from across the globe. Since our mediators were recommended by program directors, as well as being known by reputation in their regions, we believe we were able to recruit mediators widely perceived as successful leaders in their fields of practice. Once the survey was completed, we defined the qualities of an expert mediator and used the pool of mediators' survey answers to complete our research and select our panel of experts.

Characteristics of Experienced Mediators

Experienced mediators can be recognized by the number of cases mediated and their years of experience. Based on the number of cases, we divided our sample into three groups: junior mediators with less than fifty cases completed, senior mediators with between fifty and two hundred cases completed, and expert mediators with more than two hundred cases completed. Although this division is arbitrary, we feel it proposes a reasonable progression of mediators' levels of experience. As you can see in Figure 1.1, nearly half of the mediators participating in our study have completed more than five hundred mediations during their careers, with another 30 percent completing between two hundred and five hundred mediations. Thus, about 75 percent of the mediators sampled were highly experienced mediators.

Secondly, to better qualify the level of expertise of our sample, we also wanted to know how many years our mediators had been practicing. Based on the number of cases, we divided our sample into three groups: junior mediators with less than five years of experience, senior mediators with ten years of experience, and expert mediators with more than ten years of experi-

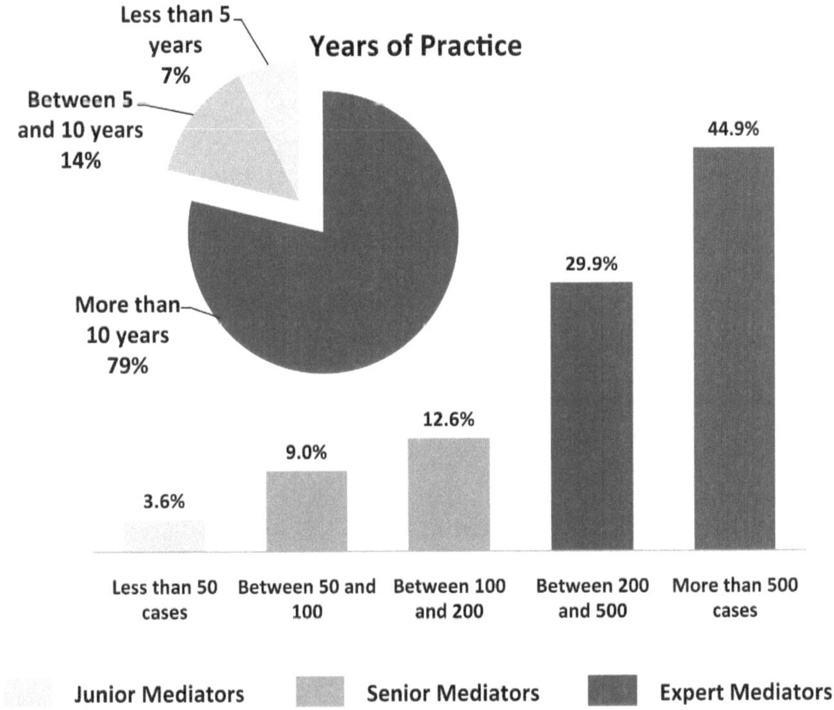

Figure 1.1. Years of experience and total career mediation cases

ence. Although this division is arbitrary, we again feel it proposes a reasonable progression of mediators' levels of experience. Figure 1.1 shows the years of practice for our sample. More than three-quarters of the mediators in our sample have practiced mediation for more than ten years, suggesting that our sample is mostly composed of expert mediators.

In addition to the number of cases and years in practice, we wanted to ensure that our sample of mediators was currently practicing mediation, rather than being retired or semiretired. This is important because the field of mediation is relatively young and continues to evolve and change swiftly. We wanted our mediators to be current in their practices. The majority of mediators in our sample mediate regularly, with 80 percent mediating at least one case per week, with the majority working more than one case per week.

Characteristics of Successful Mediators

Expert mediators are not only experienced, but also tend to have high settlement rates. Defining mediation success can be complex, and experts often disagree about the criteria that could be used to sort successful from unsuccessful mediators. Nevertheless, we decided to look at mediators' settlement rates as well as parties' satisfaction with the mediators' work. It is important to keep in mind that the data is self-reported and might be a little inflated depending on the level of social desirability of our sample (i.e., desire to look good). Based on settlement rates, we can divide our sample into three groups: below average with lower than 40 percent settlement rate, average with more than 40 percent settlement rate but less than 80 percent, and above average with a settlement rate over 80 percent. Since more than 70 percent of the mediators have a settlement rate over 80 percent, our sample seems to be mostly composed of expert mediators. Keep in mind that the type of case also impacts settlement rates. For example, employment discrimination claims have lower settlement rates than landlord/tenant cases. This factor was taken under consideration in analyzing the sample.

Seeking Diverse Backgrounds and Fields of Practice

In addition to mediators' experience, we wanted a pool of mediators with diversified backgrounds and fields of practice. Firstly, we looked at mediators' educational backgrounds as an indicator to assess diversification. As Figure 1.2 shows, the mediators in our sample come from diverse educational backgrounds, with degrees in psychology, law, social work, business, industrial relations, conflict resolution, the humanities, and the social sciences. This wide variety of education ensures that the results of the survey are not dependent on the mediators' background.

Secondly, we looked at mediators' fields of practice to assess the diversity of mediation contexts. We asked the mediators to tell us which type of mediation made up the bulk of their practices. This is important because the challenges for family mediators can be quite different than for employment or environmental mediators. Keep in mind that many of our mediators told us their mediation practices span multiple types of cases. Therefore, mediator could mark more than one category. We recognize that different countries and jurisdictions use varying terminology to refer to specific types of mediation. So, we worked hard to find the terminology that would be as clear as possible, but note that some may prefer alternative terminology.

About 48 percent of our mediators listed family and divorce mediation as their primary practice specialty. Discrimination, workplace, employment mediators comprised approximately 35 percent of our sample. Interpersonal mediation comprised approximately 25 percent of our sample. These three mediation contexts captured the bulk of the mediation practices of our participants. Figure 1.2 shows the area of practice of the mediators in our study (some mediators practice in more than one area). Consequently, the wide variety of contexts ensures that the results of the survey are not dependent on them.

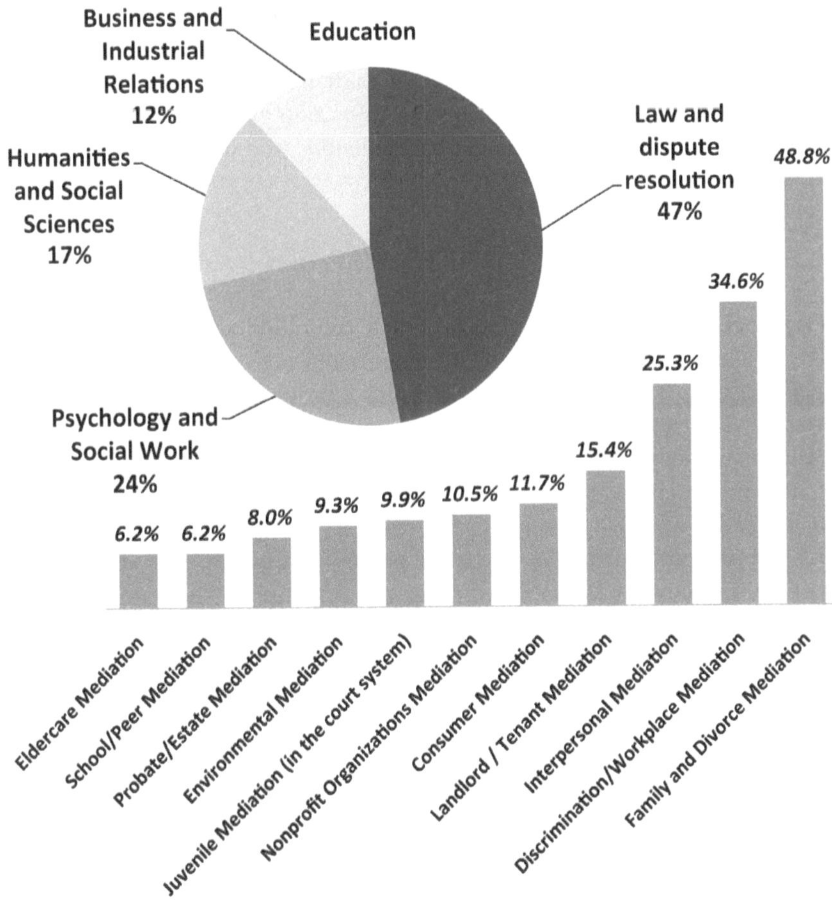

Figure 1.2. Mediator's education and fields of practice

Furthermore, our sample of mediators is almost equally divided by gender with 51 percent males and 49 percent females. However, most of our sample is composed of Caucasians (83.6 percent) while other groups are underrepresented. The lack of racial and ethnic diversity is likely to be highest among older mediators, as generational trends and governmental policies promoting diversity and workplace equality are likely to have had a greater impact on the younger generation of mediators (Hairston 1999).

Selecting Our Panel of Expert Mediators

From the sample of mediators, we constituted a pool of experts. Only mediators with over ten years of practice, more than two hundred mediated cases, and an above average settlement rate were kept in the benchmarking project.

We used statistical analysis to double-check that focusing on expert mediators would not thwart the representativeness of mediation contexts in our analysis. Using these criterions, we were able to build a subsample of eighty-five expert mediators from the pool of participants in the initial survey. While the whole sample of participants was used to pinpoint mediation challenges, only the subsample of expert mediators was used to identify best practices.

IDENTIFYING MEDIATION'S GREATEST CHALLENGES

We pinpointed mediation challenges with a two-round survey of our pool of 186 mediators over an approximate nine-month period in 2010 and 2011. Each phase of the survey was reviewed and approved by the Internal Review Board at Kennesaw State University to ensure the ethical and appropriate treatment of study participants.

The first round of surveys asked mediators to describe the three biggest challenges faced during the mediation process. This phase asked for mediators to report both difficult and frequent process challenges. Since this was an open-ended question, we received numerous responses. Afterwards, we conducted a thematic analysis in order to pull out the ten main process challenges mentioned by the mediators. Then, Phase 2 surveys asked the mediators to rank these ten challenges from most to least difficult. Subsequently, we conducted some basic quantitative analysis to sort out the most difficult challenges.

Furthermore, to make sure we had identified challenges not dependent on mediation contexts, we compared the ranking of challenges and cross-referenced by the three major mediation contexts of our sample (family/divorce mediation, discrimination/workplace mediation, and interpersonal mediation), and found all challenges were significantly difficult in all mediation contexts. As a result, we ended up with a total of eight challenges that would be present in most mediation contexts, even for expert mediators. Figure 1.3 outlines mediations' eight greatest challenges. All of these challenges can be a source of an impasse if not successfully overcome by mediators and parties. Although we believe that these challenges are common (i.e., frequent), each mediation case will likely present a variety of challenges.

Firstly, our mediators talked about the challenges posed by the fact that many parties simply do not want mediation at all. Some courts order parties to mediation, as do some employers or other referral sources. This means that mediators have to spend time explaining what mediation is and how/why it is worth trying. All of this must occur before the mediator can get to the actual dispute. The work of educating parties about the mediation process and persuading them to engage in it can be as difficult as the mediation itself.

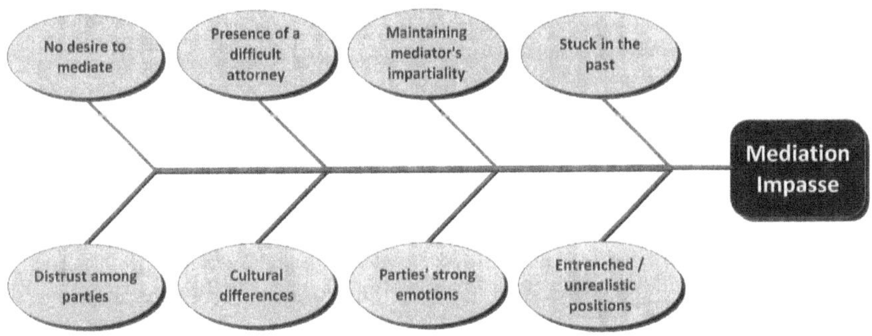

Figure 1.3. Mediation's greatest challenges

Secondly, parties come to mediation because something has gone wrong. Somewhere along the line, at least one party has not behaved the way the other party expected them to act. Trust has been damaged. Yet in order for mediation to end in an agreement, the parties must have some renewed trust that the other(s) will fulfill that agreement. For these reasons, distrust among parties is an important mediation challenges.

Next, the presence of attorneys can be crucial in moving the negotiations along smoothly. Attorneys can offer legal advice, provide strong reality checks to their clients, and clarify the differences between a party's emotional desires and a true legal argument. When an attorney understands the mediation process and its possible benefits, he/she is a real asset to the mediator. Unfortunately, not all attorneys get it. For this reason, dealing with attorneys also presents challenges, with our mediators ranking it as the fifth mediation challenge. It is worth a quick reminder that nearly half of the mediators in our sample are attorneys themselves.

Fourthly, dealing with cultural differences can be quite challenging. Our mediators noted that linguistic differences are the tip of the iceberg when it comes to the challenges posed by intercultural mediation. The deepest challenges stemmed from different meanings ascribed to behaviors, nonverbal communication, gender, and other role expectation differences. And the biggest part of the cultural challenge is that it is hard to know what you do not know, leaving many cultural miscommunications unaddressed.

Next, in spite of their best efforts to remain wholly impartial, mediators do sometimes find themselves reaching opinions about the case and the parties. Our own experiences, biases, and preferences can creep into the mediation room when we least expect them. Our mediators provided some good advice about how to maintain neutrality and impartiality, even with difficult parties.

Sixthly, mediators ranked dealing with emotions as a challenge to the mediation process. A lack of emotional control, hot tempers, and flaring hostility can easily lead a party to walk away from the process. Yet some of our mediators noted that the absence or withholding of emotional expressions can also sabotage the mediation process. A common denominator for successful mediators is that they learn to be comfortable with the expression of both strong and buried emotions and to help parties harness emotions for the benefit of conflict resolution.

Seventhly, the moment when the discussions turn from what happened in the past to how will we build a better future is pivotal. When parties are unable to make the turn from a past to future focus, they are usually unable to reach an agreement and the case ends in an impasse. For this reason, our mediators ranked moving from a focus on the past to the future as the fourth mediation challenge.

Finally, dealing with entrenched and unrealistic expectations is also an important challenge faced by the mediators in our study. They found that parties frequently arrived at mediation with a my way or the highway attitude or they had a specific number or position stuck in their mind and would not entertain other possible dollar amount or options. Persuading parties to really listen to each other, to withhold final judgment until all information had been shared, and to brainstorm a list of potential elements in a resolution can be impossible when parties remain entrenched in their original positions.

LEARNING FROM EXPERT MEDIATORS

Having identified mediation's greatest challenges, the next step is to flesh out the best practices to overcome these challenges. We used a benchmarking framework to increase the validity and transferability of our findings. It was important to us that any proposed practice was not based on our opinion, but rather from the collective wisdom of our panel of expert mediators. While each mediator may have his or her own trick to deal with a challenge, we wanted to focus on the common best practices. Thus we were looking for the preferred strategies of our panel. In addition, we made sure to include a diverse background of mediation practice to make sure that the identified practices would be applicable in all mediation contexts. Our benchmarking process can be divided into four steps.

First, we constituted a panel of expert mediators to benchmark the best practices. We invited each of the 101 identified expert mediators in our subsample to participate in another survey to identify how to resolve the eight greatest mediation challenges. Given the fact that this second survey was likely to be time consuming, a total of eighty-five mediators accepted to participate. We double-checked that our panel of expert mediators was still representative of the diversity of mediation contexts. The short biographies of our panel of experts are presented in Appendix 1.

Second, we asked our panel of experts to split challenges into potential root causes, to describe their preferred strategies to overcome these challenges, and to give a concrete example of how they would use the strategies. To make sure our results would be valid and transferable, we did not want to limit ourselves to building a list of strategies. We wanted to split challenges according to their root causes as we suspected that strategies may vary depending on root causes. We also wanted to have examples of how each strategy was used to better flesh out the best practices.

Third, we conducted an analysis in order to pull out common themes. For each challenge, common root causes were categorized and best practices were fleshed out. As a result, we were able to build a mindmap of how expert mediators diagnose the root causes of each challenge. Moreover, we were also able to elaborate on the best practices with real life examples using our panel of experts' cases. We used probability analysis to match root causes with the best practices to identify the preferred strategies for each situation.

Finally, we discussed the application of each best practice in regards to timing and risk management. Using our panel of experts' insights, as well as the mediation literature, we also looked at the proper mediation context in regards to the use of a strategy. In some cases, timing is crucial to the efficient use of a best practice. Furthermore, we discussed the potential risks and risk mitigation strategies for each best practice. As a result, the transferability of each best practice was enhanced.

This benchmarking process has been applied to the eight mediation challenges. In the next chapters, mediation's greatest challenges will be exposed, their root causes will be diagnosed and the preferred best practices to overcome them will be fleshed out. In each chapter, an emphasis is put on the validity and transferability of our findings.

Chapter Two

Dealing with Resistance to Mediation

If talking was going to fix this problem, it would have been fixed by now.

I don't want to be in the same room as that jerk. Now I am expected to talk to him face-to-face?!

I've been litigating cases like this for ten years. Why should I be forced to take my clients to mediation now, when I know I can win in court?!

Even for expert mediators, getting both parties to the mediation table is sometimes the biggest struggle. Parties, and sometimes their attorneys, have many reasons why they do not want to try mediation. Sometimes all parties seek to avoid mediation, while in other cases one party wants to give it a try but they cannot get the other side onboard. Mediators worldwide complain about no-shows and cancellations that make scheduling their work and maintaining a steady income fairly difficult. Mediators and mediation program administrators find themselves repeatedly explaining the various benefits of the mediation process and seeking to convince parties to keep an open mind and give it a try.

Sometimes mediation is completely voluntary and self-referred. In other cases, the parties are required to attend mediation but not required to reach a settlement. Even when parties are ordered to appear for mediation, this does not mean they will keep an open mind and truly give the process a try. As the saying goes, you can lead a horse to water, but you can't make him drink. One expert mediator wrote, "Getting over the first hurdle can be the hardest." The first step in any successful mediation is to get the parties to commit to showing up for mediation.

Even experienced mediators get frustrated by parties who do not want to mediate, sometimes even in the face of a judge's order to do so. Experienced mediators understand the benefits of the process and have seen it work, even with parties who were initially cynical about its prospects. Yet mediation cannot work if the parties do not come to the table and agree to give mediation a try. For this reason, dealing with parties who do not want to mediate remains a significant challenge.

Experienced, successful mediators have found ways of dealing with cases in which one or both parties do not want to mediate. This chapter will examine the reasons why parties may be reluctant to get involved in mediation. Then we will examine strategies used to overcome resistance to mediation and share mediator success stories.

WHY SOME PARTIES DO NOT WANT TO MEDIATE

We asked mediators to be specific about the reasons why dealing with parties reluctant to mediate can be a challenge. A humorous story from mediator Jerry Wood illustrates on how the beginning of mediation can be touchy with reluctant parties:

> A crusty older gentleman sat down at the mediation table and pronounced that he knew that the lawyer for the other side was a crook and that he believed that both the judge and the mediator were in his pocket. The lawyer just smiled and said nothing. I said something to the effect of, "Well gentlemen the court has ordered you to mediate, but I can't proceed if either one of you objects to my neutrality in this case. Perhaps you would rather reschedule with a different mediator." The gentleman said, "That wouldn't do any good because you are all a bunch of crooks." I stated, "Ok, what do you gentlemen want to do." The lawyer said, "The court ordered us here, let's just get it over with." "Fine with me," answered the gentleman. I then proceeded as usual, and the parties reached a complete settlement. The crusty gentleman said, "I'm not really satisfied, but this is better than I would have got from that crooked judge."

According to expert mediators, there are many reasons parties prefer not to mediate their cases. The most common reasons are hopelessness or fearfulness, a misunderstanding or mistrust of the mediation process, and an unwillingness to settle (see Figure 2.1).

Parties Feel Hopeless or Fearful

According to our mediators, the most common reason to be resistant to mediation is related to a feeling of hopelessness that the dispute cannot be resolved cooperatively. Sometimes this hopelessness includes fear of being taken advantage of by the other party or a concern that the other party will

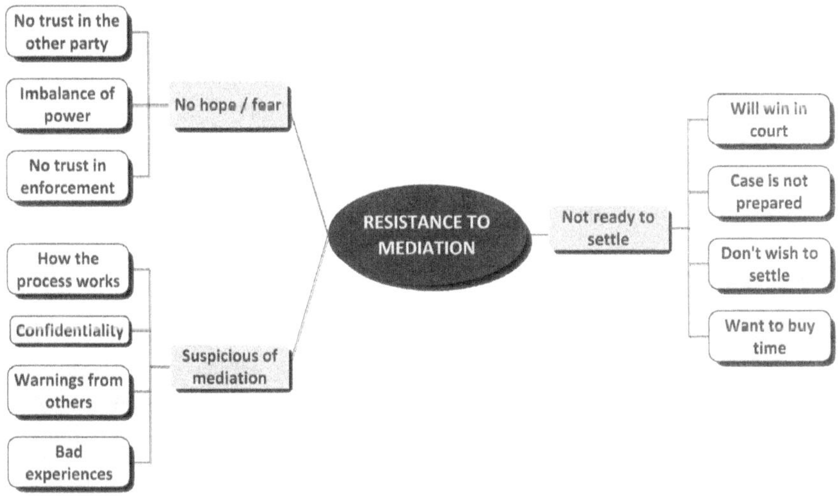

Figure 2.1. Mind map of reasons why parties may be reluctant to mediate

not mediate in good faith or fulfill agreements. In addition, many of our mediators told us that power imbalances often leave one side fearful of participating in mediation, where they might feel coerced to settle or feel outmatched by the other side. Mediator Marry Kelleher-Forsyth summarizes this point: "The party who does not want to mediate may feel the other party has more power and will therefore be in control of the process and will win no matter what the first party says or does in mediation."

In some cases, one party may feel physically or emotionally intimidated by the presence or behavior of the other party. As a result, the first party might prefer to meet only in court or have the attorneys negotiate a settlement on their behalf. Mediator Susan V. Edwards illustrates this point,

> Participating in mediation without an attorney can be really intimidating to people who have been on the wrong end of that imbalance during the marriage. [It is] difficult to believe that one person [the mediator] will be able to keep that person under control. While allowing the attorneys to sit in or be available at any time can offer some reassurance, I think a lot of these people have lost any confidence they may have once had in their ability to handle differences of opinion, verbal abuse, stand up for themselves, or even their own ability to make decisions.

Finally, parties may want to know the extent to which agreements are legally binding due to fears that one side will make, but not keep, the agreement. As mediator Karena Ellis-Greenway points out, "Parties want a legal agreement in the courts as they feel the other party will renege on any agreement if not put in place by a judge or court." Depending upon the institutional context within which a mediation occurs (or lack thereof), the agreement may or may not be binding and enforceable in court like a judge's order. In most court-connected mediation, agreements are enforceable as court orders once the judge signs off on them. However, many individual elements within a mediation agreement may be difficult or impossible to enforce since they deal with practical rather than legal matters (e.g., the parties agree to avoid using put-downs when they speak to each other).

Parties Misunderstand Mediation

For most parties, the word mediation still gets confused with meditation. The average consumer, tenant, or divorcing parent has only a vague notion of what mediation is, if they have any notion at all. Some parties see Court TV, which is really arbitration, but they believe they understand court proceedings.

Furthermore, mediation is not a highly publicized process. Parties may not only have a poor understanding of the process, but they may be unaware of its potential as a dispute resolution strategy. As mediator Julie K. Pinkus reports, "There is a lack of knowledge about how successful mediation can be and a failure to see the advantages of mediating." Because mediation is a confidential process and parties are asked to keep the negotiations private, word does not get out at the same rate as other forms of dispute resolution. As mediator David Lichter points out, "People who are unfamiliar with a process can often distrust it. This is particularly true with the disclosure of very confidential information."

Sometimes, the lack of knowledge and information about mediation breeds mistrust and suspicion. Parties in an ongoing dispute may be in a state of financial or psychological stress, making them less likely to trust that a stranger can sit down and help them with their problems. Mediators also noted that a negative mediation experience tends to be shared more broadly by word of mouth than a positive experience. As mediator Mary Kelleher-Forsyth states, "They either do not understand the mediation process or have heard bad things about it from someone whose opinion they trust." In some cases, this suspicion can also be grounded in past disappointing mediation experiences.

Not Ready to Settle

There are a number of reasons why parties may not be ready to settle. Firstly, they may believe they will prevail in court and they are willing to deal with the transaction costs involved. As mediator Alan Gross points out, "If there is a power imbalance, the more powerful party such as the boss or the parent may wish to resolve a conflict by fiat or force. Powerful parties may not feel the need to negotiate or mediate." They may also be suffering from what is often called, *jackpot syndrome*, meaning they have an unrealistically high evaluation of how their case will fare in court.

Secondly, some parties do not know how to prepare for mediation, what to bring, how long the process will take, the background of the mediator, and what to expect. In the face of so many unknowns it is simply easier to skip mediation altogether. As one of our expert mediators summarizes, "It happens most often in pro se situations, where the anti-mediation party has an unrealistic expectation that they will get what they want through a method other than mediation, and they do not have anyone who they trust to provide information that may challenge that idea."

Thirdly, some parties may not see the value of settling the conflict. Sometimes the status quo works more to the benefit of one side than the other. In other cases, a party may have a conflict avoidant personality tendency that makes him or her seek to avoid the direct acknowledgement that a problem exists and must be faced head-on. In cases such as divorce, settlement may mean there will be little or no future contact between the parties and one side may not be ready to say good-bye to the relationship. Remaining entrenched in conflict is one way to maintain contact with the other side. There are many reasons why one or even both sides may resist settlement in general, and therefore mediation as a means of settlement. For instance, mediator Timothy Hedeen points out that "[Parties may have] a low investment in a relationship or a dispute." According to mediator Andy G. Miller, "Sometimes they have a matter they do not wish to settle or that it does not make any sense for them to settle."

Lastly, in some cases stalling is the optimal strategy for one or more parties. For example, an employee may become more desperate the longer she is unemployed. Companies may prefer to delay the resolution of wrongful termination cases with the belief that the employee will settle for less the longer the case drags on. Similarly, in divorce cases, eventually one party will likely want to remarry and will be more generous in the settlement negotiations in order to get the divorce finalized. Stalling or delaying the resolution process may be a tactical way to achieve one's goals, even if that means rescheduling mediation multiple times.

STRATEGIES TO DEAL WITH RESISTANCE TO MEDIATION

Dealing with parties who do not want to mediate is a frequent challenge, even for expert mediators. Getting parties involved in mediation is rarely automatic. Fortunately, mediators have a number of techniques and approaches they employ with parties who are hesitant or outright against mediation. These strategies are explaining mediation, reminding the parties they are under no obligation to settle the case, exploring the parties' concerns, and engaging the mediation process.

Explaining Mediation

By far, the most frequent strategy used by the mediators in our study was to explain mediation to the parties. While most parties and cases benefit from mediation, not all do. Therefore, it is important and only fair for parties to have the full and complete information about the mediation process: its costs and benefits, alternatives to mediation, the enforceability of any agreements made, and to have assurances of the confidential nature of the mediation process. Only then can parties and their attorneys reach educated decisions about whether mediation is worth trying for their cases. Explaining the mediation process is crucial to building trust and rapport between the mediator and the parties. If mediators try to skip it or rush through it, parties may bolt.

How Mediators Explain Mediation

Several aspects of the mediation process can be explained to the parties. The key is to take the time necessary to build the parties' familiarity with the process. As mediator Daniel E. Gulden states, "[There should not be any] rushing through the mediator's opening so as to address any misunderstandings." Taking time to answer all questions about the process is important. Mediator Alan Gross concurs: "[I provide a] careful and clear explanation of the process before the parties come to the table as well as in the opening statement, followed by transparent responses to all concerns or questions."

Secondly, expert mediators stress the characteristics of mediation to build trust in the process and mediators outline their roles as guardians of the process. Mediator Evan A. Ash gives the example "[I] attempt to reduce resistance by encouraging to promise of the process—balance, neutrality, empowerment, etc." In addition, our mediators focused specifically on the need for parties to be reassured about the confidential nature of the proceedings. This may be especially important in workplace and business disputes, where reputations are critical to a party's ability to move forward with his or her life once the dispute has been resolved. Mediator David Lichter "[I] reassure the party concerning the confidential nature of the mediation, and I mention the protections that the applicable statutes and rules provide." Some mediators will put all this information in writing when parties are still wary about the process. An expert mediator illustrates this strategy: "[I prepare] a protocol agreement that spells out [the parties'] rights and protections."

Then, expert mediators will emphasize the benefits of mediation to finalize their explanation of the process. In order to assess the costs and benefits of mediation, parties need to know how much mediation is likely to cost (if anything), and be able to compare these financial and nonfinancial costs to other resolution process options such as litigation or arbitration. This may come across as somewhat of a reality check, forcing them to weigh the costs of continuing the conflict until adjudication or leaving it unresolved indefinitely. For example, mediator Karena Ellis-Greenway uses a cost-benefit frame, "I try to explain the benefits and the potential costs if taken to the law courts." On the other hand, mediator Julie K. Pinkus stresses risks versus control, "[I] educate the person about the risks associated with going to court versus having control over their compromises at mediation."

When Mediators Explain Mediation

Ideally, parties should receive information about the mediation process from the program staff, their attorneys, or others who are involved with the intake and scheduling of cases. Private practice mediators often must take on all of these tasks, including sending out emails or pamphlets that explain the mediation process, the role of the mediator, and answer frequently asked questions. When parties do not feel they are ready to settle or mediate, explaining the mediation process is often the key to initiating a mediation. An expert mediator gives an example of how this strategy can work to get parties to start a mediation: "Two parties did not want to use an interest based process, so we crafted a protocol agreement that limited the number of meetings and spelled out confidentiality. In the end, they liked the process, ignored their self-imposed limit on the number of sessions, and got a deal."

Sometimes mediators have to show patience when reluctant parties are suspicious about mediation. This is especially true when one party is contacted by a mediator who has been approached by the other party. Mediator Barbara Wilson tells a wonderful story that illustrates how patience and explanation can help a party overcome resistance to mediation:

> I was approached by a father (referred by his solicitor) who wanted to mediate with his ex-wife concerning parenting agreements for their son. When I contacted her, she was suspicious of why he had approached me and not someone else, was I acting as his agent, how I could understand the situation without reading the very large legal files, and [the purpose of mediation when] her solicitor was confident that she would win at court. I dealt with this by explaining that I'm an independent practitioner but of course they could go to another mediator if she preferred and her ex-husband agreed. I said I understood she needed time to think and seek legal advice, that it was her decision, and that I would be happy to answer any questions. I asked her to let me know what she wanted to do within an agreed upon period and explained I wouldn't contact her before then. I then asked her open questions about domestic abuse (there wasn't any) and speculated, "I guess you're moving on with your life?" She said, "yes," but this was hanging over her and she didn't want to go to court. I explained this was a potential opportunity for her to take another step

> forward and also to avoid court proceedings, but again emphasized that it was her decision. I gave her time to reflect and ended the call after a reasonable duration: long enough to connect with her and answer her questions, but not long enough for her to feel harassed. She rang back the next day and agreed to mediate with certain provisions about the location, and confirmed she'd take legal advice in the meantime.

Risks of Explaining Mediation

Not only is it the mediator's core duty to explain the process and his or her role, it could be considered malpractice or a breach of ethics to refrain from doing so. It is crucial for mediators and program staffers to provide information about the mediation process before parties arrive for mediation, if at all possible. In addition, there is little to no risk in explaining the mediation process, and this phase of the mediation can be used to build rapport through the transparent sharing of information and party concerns. However, a frequent mistake is to believe that the mediator's opening statement is enough. It is important to keep in mind that parties often need multiple explanations, re-explanations, or reminders about the mediation process and the role of the mediator. These may occur before and during the mediation sessions.

Stressing the Non-obligation to Settle

When mediators explain the process to parties, they often put extra emphasis on the fact that there is no obligation to settle the case in mediation. The goal of explaining mediation is to build trust in the process, and the objective of stressing the non-obligation to settle is in order to minimize the perceived risk of trying out mediation. Once parties understand they are in control of the outcome of the case, they usually have fewer fears and a greater willingness to proceed. If parties begin to feel pressured to settle they may feel reassured by a reminder about the voluntary nature of reaching agreements.

How Mediators Explain there Is No Obligation to Settle

Explaining to parties that there is no obligation to reach a settlement can take many forms. First, mediators can explain what mandatory mediation is; the objective is to make clear that parties are required to try to solve their dispute through mediation but are not required to reach a settlement. Parties who are ordered to attend mediation by the courts, their employer, a homeowners' association, or due to an alternative dispute resolution (ADR) clause in a commercial contract, are under no obligation to reach an agreement in mediation. An expert mediator gives the example, "[I] explain that there is no requirement to come to [a] resolution, only requesting a good faith effort to talk and hear each other out. Going to court always remains an option."

Parties need to understand that their obligations are fulfilled when they appear for mediation and allow the process to proceed.

Secondly, mediators can explain their role and stress that they have no power to force a solution. Mediators help parties regain a sense of control by reminding them that they control the outcome in mediation. Mediator Jerome A. Diekemper states, "I emphasize self-determination and the lack of power of the neutral to force any party to do anything the party does not want to do. I suggest that people strongly consider doing what they ultimately judge to be in their own best interests."

Thirdly, mediators can play down mediation as compared to court proceedings. Mediators remind parties and attorneys that if mediation fails to result in settlement, they still have all the same options they had before. This is the nothing to lose argument. As mediator Henry W. Kimmel simply puts it, "[I] tell them at the very least that mediation is a dress rehearsal for trial."

When Mediators Explain Parties Have No Obligation to Settle

Expert mediators stress the fact that there is no obligation to settle when parties misunderstand or are suspicious of the mediation process. An expert mediator illustrates this strategy with a small claim mediation example:

> I was mediating in landlord/tenant court. The judge sent a *pro se* case out for mediation. Once in the room for mediation, the tenant said that she wasn't interested. I asked her why. She said that she didn't think her landlord would give her what she wanted. I let her know that based on what the judge said when everyone was in the courtroom, cases where there was not an agreement and no lawyers were saved for last. If she went back into the courtroom at that time, she would likely be sitting on the bench, waiting. I asked her if she would like to try to spend her time trying to resolve the situation in mediation instead. I reminded her that she could leave at any time if she found the mediation not to be working. She agreed to stay.

Stressing the fact that an agreement is not mandatory is also often used to convince parties who feel they have been forced to mediate to give it a try. For an example, mediator John Settle's story illustrates how this strategy can be used to engage parties in the mediation process:

> In Small Claims Court, both parties have been summarily ordered by a judge to participate, and they were resistant and angry about that. I began by recognizing their concerns [and] asking them to let me describe the process and its safeguards [no obligation to settle]. Giving a good, confident description, coupled with the suggestion like "let's start and see how it goes," influenced them to try it, and we proceeded to discuss and resolve the matter.

Risks of Explaining there is No Obligation to Settle

Providing process information is generally of low risk, especially when it puts the power and control back into the hands of the parties. Since the alternative is an impasse, there is little to be lost by attempting to explain the benefits of mediation to a reluctant party. However, there may be some risks entailed when one side feels the mediator is spending too much time dealing with the other side's fears about mediation, especially if the hourly rate is split between the parties.

EXPLORING CONCERNS

Parties may be knowledgeable of the mediation process and trust the mediator, but still have concerns about the process. They may have concerns about meeting the other party face-to-face, the confidentiality of the discussion, or that mediation will fit their procedural needs, such as avoiding being insulted again by the other party. Concerns can be explored at any phase of the process, although it is most efficient to do so as early as possible. It is most efficient if all concerns are shared in the beginning phase and explored together.

How Mediators Explore Concerns

The basic strategy expert mediators use to explore concerns is to simply have the parties voice them and then talk about them. Mediators ask open-ended questions in order to discover the needs and interests that underlie the concerns. Mediator Mary Kelleher-Forsyth illustrates this strategy: "I will explain the process to them give examples of how mediation might deal with their issues or concern. I start a conversation with them about their concerns and work towards relieving them. I may or may not include the other party in the conversation."

In addition, mediators need to express genuine interest in the parties concerns, normalize fears and reservations, and refrain from delegitimizing the parties' perspectives, while sharing factual information about the pros and cons of mediation. One expert mediator said, "[I] give parties all the time they need to ask questions, acknowledge that they are feeling a lack of trust with me and/or the mediation process, talk about why, and ask if there is anything I can do to address that lack of trust."

When Mediators Explore Concerns

Exploring concerns is done when one or both parties have no confidence in resolving the case through mediation. The objective in such cases is to show parties how mediation can help them. As mediator Robert Martell's example shows, exploring and responding to concerns can help parties decide to try mediation:

> Neighbors hadn't spoken together for 7 years over a boundary/fence dispute. I was referred by an enlightened solicitor and I spent several hours in face-to-face pre-mediation meetings explaining the process and reassuring them that I would manage the process sensitively and that they wouldn't have to face each other if they chose not to on the day of mediation. I understood that they both said the dispute was draining and stressful on a daily basis so I invited them to consider what life would be like without this problem. Could they imagine being in a place where there was no dispute and no anxiety when they walked into their gardens. They found it difficult to imagine it but both wanted it so badly that they put their trust in me to help them resolve it.

When parties are fearful of meeting each other, exploring their concerns can help mediators design a process that will make the parties more comfortable. The objective is to show that mediation can be adapted to their concerns. Mediator Alan Gross illustrates this strategy with the following case:

> In a recent workplace mediation, a supervisor was concerned that elements of her participation in the session would be leaked to her Board of Directors. I prepared a confidentiality agreement for both parties and also pledged that I would keep everything that occurred in the session confidential except any agreements that they mutually wished to release or share.

Risks of Exploring Concerns

Exploring the parties' concerns, displaying empathy, and maintaining transparency about the costs and benefits of mediation are low risk activities. Most concerns can be met through the supply of information about the mediation process and a party's self-determination. However, it is important to remember that mediation rests on the pillar of self-determination. Therefore, if a mediator presses too hard to get a party to agree to mediate, this behavior may be perceived as coercive. If one or more parties are offended by the mediator's pressure to mediate, and depending upon the rules of the specific mediation program or venue, a party has the right to file an ethics complaint against the mediator. The goal is to explore the parties' concerns and supply information without crossing the line into coercion. Where the line is drawn depends upon the parties, their attorneys, and the mediator—and they may not be in agreement about where to draw the line.

ENGAGING THE PROCESS

Mediators often fall back on the simplicity and utility of the mediation process itself to convince parties to stay in mediation. The basic principle is to let parties start the process and see how it goes. Once the mediation gets started, momentum is built and parties become engaged in the process; thus they might be reluctant to stop. As mediator Jerry Wood puts it, "By the time we engage in problem solving, the parties are usually invested in the process."

How Mediators Engage the Process

Strategies to engage parties can take many forms. Firstly, mediators can ask parties to give it a try. Mediators will mention the importance of starting the process while acknowledging parties' emotional needs, cynicism, and reticence. It is important to build trust and rapport while refraining from criticizing the party's fears and reservations. Mediator David Lichter gives the example, "I will discuss with the reluctant party that many times people will come into a mediation thinking that a matter will never settle and it does, so that the party should give the process a chance. I try to make sure the person stays engaged throughout the process."

Secondly, mediators frequently remind hesitant parties they have little to risk by attempting mediation—if it does not work, they can proceed with the case in whatever manner they would have chosen if mediation had never occurred. The objective is to give control to parties so they trust the process more. Mediators can offer for parties to stop mediation when they feel it is going nowhere. Mediator Daniel E. Gulden illustrates this point: "[I] assure them that they are free to terminate the session at any time but request that they just give it a fair chance to see if progress, for their benefit, can be achieved."

When Mediators Engage the Process

When parties are suspicious of mediation, expert mediators will sometimes ask parties to give mediation a chance with the possibility to stop the process later. Usually, once parties see things moving forward, they become engaged in mediation. Mediator Jerry Wood gives an example that illustrates how starting mediation builds momentum:

> In a personal injury case, both sides said that mediation would be a waste of time and that they were only there because the court had a standing order for mediation. I asked everyone if they were willing to give the process a try. Once we broke into caucuses, each party lowered his defenses and engaged in a discussion about relative strengths and weaknesses of his case.

Sometimes, using a caucus to start the process is necessary when a joint meeting would be bluntly ineffective. In such cases, the goal is still to build momentum. As mediator John Settle relates,

> A complainant refused to be in the presence or direct influence of the other party. We all agreed to start mediation in private sessions with both parties, on the condition that we thereafter [would] reassess how to proceed. This engagement led to the complainant's agreement to a joint session, based on better information about the process and trust in me.

Risks of Engaging the Process

There are few risks of engaging the process and redirecting parties' attentions from the outcome back to the process itself. When parties arrive at the mediation session, they are often anxious about the process and fearful of the outcome. Mediators can reassure them by inviting them to take it one step at a time, and reminding them that no outcome will be reached without their consent. Parties need to be aware they can terminate mediation at any time without reaching an agreement. The biggest risk, from the parties' standpoint, is that time may be wasted on a process that may or may not result in an agreement they feel they can accept. Since most paid mediators have a minimum charge (e.g., a fee for at least one or two hours of service) for cases which settle or impasse quickly, parties might need to be reminded that there is no extra cost for engaging in the process as long as the time is covered by the minimum charge.

SUMMARY

Getting parties to the metaphorical mediation table and gaining their willing participation is sometimes the most difficult challenge for mediators. We certainly cannot mediate without the parties' presence and input. While some parties are ordered to attend mediation by their boss, a human resource manager, or a judge, many others come to mediation voluntarily. Mediators who work in both voluntary and mandatory mediation programs feel the difference in the parties' attitudes and perspectives when parties enter the room. Therefore, all mediators must be able to fully explain the mediation process, explore parties concerns and reservations, explain there is little risk in attempting to mediate the case since settlement is not required, and encourage parties to start the process. This requires mediators to use their skills even before the process officially starts in order to meet the parties' needs for information, control, and a transparent process. Table 2.1 below summarizes strategies used by mediators to deal with parties' resistance to mediation.

Table 2.1. Summary of Strategies to Deal with Parties Who Do Not Want to Mediate

STRATEGIES	HOW?	WHEN?	RISK?
Explaining Mediation	*- Explain process* *- Explain mediator's role* *- Explain mediation safeguards* *- Explain benefits of mediation*	*- Parties are not ready to settle*	*- Believe opening statement is enough*
Stressing the Non-obligation to Settle	*- Explain mandatory mediation* *- Explain the role of the mediator* *- Play down mediation*	*- Misunderstanding or mistrust in the mediation process*	*- Appear to be taking sides*
Exploring Concerns	*- Have parties voice their concerns* *- Adapt the process*	*- No hope to achieve results*	*- Appear to be taking sides*
Engaging the Process	*- Ask parties to give mediation a try* *- Stress the option to stop mediation later*	*- Misunderstanding or mistrust in the mediation process*	*- Appear to be taking sides*

Chapter Three

Dealing with Mistrust among Parties

Why should I believe anything she says?

There is no point in reaching an agreement. He never keeps his promises.

I have no interest in working with him to find a solution. I would rather take my chances with the judge.

Many, but not all, of the disputes that we see in mediation involve issues of mistrust. A party may believe that the other has behaved inappropriately in the past, and therefore lacks trust that the other party will behave differently in the future. Even if no breach of trust has occurred, in order for a party to reach an agreement in mediation, he or she must have some level of trust that the agreement will be implemented. Thus, at some level, trust comes into play with most mediation. The more severe the distrust between parties, the more difficult it is to reach an agreement.

Mistrust between disputants poses a myriad of challenges to the mediation process: from getting the parties to come to the table, a willingness to share concerns openly, to the commitment and implementation of agreements. The entire mediation process is at risk when distrust poisons the relationship between parties. For example, mistrust between parties makes them less willing to attend mediation unless they are compelled by a court, the mandatory alternative dispute resolution (ADR) clauses in employment contracts, or similar coercive mechanisms that require participation in mediation. Sometimes, a party does not want to sit across the table from the other party due to the residual anger or frustration stemming from perceived breaches of norms and expectations.

In addition, mistrust makes parties reticent to share information fully. They may fear that the other side will use that information in subsequent litigation or share it with others involved in the dispute. An unwillingness to openly discuss needs and interests makes it harder to reach a resolution in mediation and makes integrative bargaining impossible. Lastly, when trust is lacking between parties, they are less willing to commit to an agreement. They may fear that the other party will not fulfill his or her commitments, therefore making agreements worthless.

As a result, mistrust between parties may jeopardize the initiation of mediation or lead to an impasse during the process. Experienced mediators have found ways of dealing with parties' mistrust in order to help parties progress, solve problems, and reach resolutions. This chapter will examine the reasons why parties might mistrust each other by breaking down the various root causes of mistrust. Then we will examine strategies used to overcome mistrust between parties, and share mediator success stories.

WHY DO PARTIES MISTRUST EACH OTHER?

We asked mediators to be specific about the reasons why parties might come to mistrust each other. Although mistrust can result from a single event, it is usually the result of a culmination of smaller events. A explanation from mediator Don Greenstein will help to illustrate how mistrust builds up between parties.

> Usually the disagreement has festered for a long time so there is no trust between the parties, so there is an assumption that the past actions of the parties will continue rather than gaining trust that the parties are capable of being trusted and working together toward a new mutual understanding.

For various reasons, parties might end up having low or no trust with which to proceed successfully in mediation. Our panel of mediators gave us four main reasons why parties might mistrust each other: a history of disappointment, a fear of being taken advantage of, an anticipation of bad behavior from the other party, and a misunderstanding of mediation (see Figure 3.1).

History of Disappointment

Our panel of expert mediators has proposed three main reasons why parties might have a history of disappointment. First, mediators indicated that some parties come into mediation having already established a pattern of promise breaking with the result being high levels of distrust. As mediator Don Greenstein puts it, "The relationship has broken down over time and the parties won't give each other the benefit of the doubt." Second, parties may

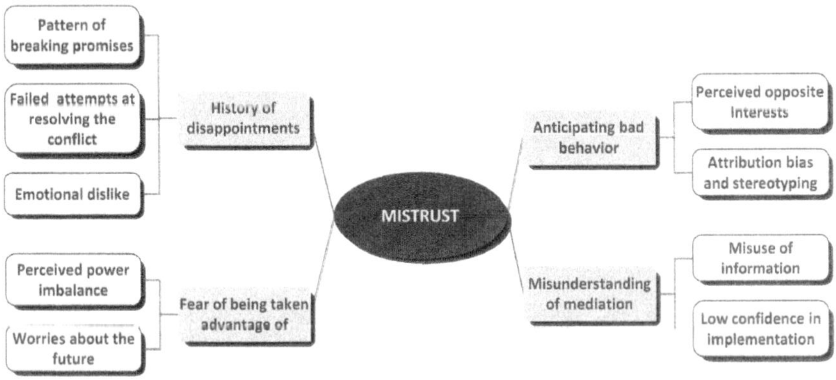

Figure 3.1. Mind map of reasons why parties might mistrust each other

have developed mistrust after repeated unsuccessful efforts to settle the dispute, leaving them feeling jaded against both the other party and the likelihood of settlement itself. Mediator Julie Barnes agrees that "[Parties] don't think that it can be successful, sometimes because of past failed attempts to work things out with the other party."

In family and workplace mediation, the disputes between parties have usually had a long time to grow and change. Understandably, parties base their future predictions of the other's behavior upon past actions. This long and checkered relationship history means they come to the mediation table with heavy baggage and sometimes voice their frustrations with the mediator since he or she cannot fully understand the history of perceived bad behavior. In such cases, any small thing, a perceived slight or sign of disrespect from the other party, can result in the end of mediation.

Finally, mistrust between parties may be worsened by personality conflicts and genuine dislike. Sometimes, the parties simply weigh values differently or have different perspectives on an issue but have been unable or unwilling to view the other's perspective as equally valid. As mediator Steven J. Gold puts it, "[Mistrust] may be real, based on a history. It may be exaggerated based upon emotional dislike."

Fear of being Taken Advantage of

In many ways, parties are often fearful that they will be taken advantage of by the other party. Parties may feel vulnerable to the actions, statements, or betrayals of the other side, therefore preferring to avoid the party altogether. As a result, parties may experience anxiety, depression, or fear at the thought of interacting with the other party. Such apprehension may lead to a learned desire of avoidance. Numerous factors can explain why parties fear exploitation.

First, one or more parties may fear being taken advantage of due to a real or perceived imbalance of power. The lower-power party may fear that mediation will result in a coerced settlement or that his or her rights will be less protected than if the dispute was resolved by an authoritative decision maker. According to mediator Tony Newport, "[Parties] are afraid they cannot control the outcome so they are reluctant to be first to take a risk." A second reason might be the fear of not being able to monitor the implementation of the agreement. According to mediator Bruce Engelbert, "[Parties may have] concerns about unforeseen events complicating agreement implementation."

It is important to keep in mind that some cases are better off going to court than mediation, especially when a party needs to be protected from predatory or discriminatory behaviors that may not be amenable to resolution in mediation. If one or more parties are likely to continue to engage in criminal or predatory behaviors, then mediation may be insufficient to resolve the dispute. While this is the case for a minority of disputes, mediators must be cognizant of the fact that palpable fear and mistrust on the part of one party may signal a need to dig deeper to discern whether mediation is the appropriate dispute resolution process.

Anticipating Bad Behaviors

Many parties assume the worst about the others' intentions and future actions, and this leads to an unwillingness to mediate, as well as to higher rates of impasse once parties get to the mediation table. In addition to perceived dishonesty, several factors can lead to anticipating bad behaviors.

Right or wrong, parties often assume that the interests of the other party contradict their own. As mediator Julie Barnes states, "[Parties] assume that the other party's interest is directly opposed to their own." This can become a form of cognitive bias that makes it difficult for negotiators to accurately assess and weigh offers and counteroffers. However, in some cases, a party is correct in believing that the other party intends to behave badly in the future and derail the implementation of the agreement. It is not always possible for the mediator to know which situation is at hand.

In addition, parties frequently engage in attribution bias and stereotyping. Attribution bias occurs when parties make assumptions about the other's motives, future behavior, and values. Sometimes the parties have never sat down and discussed the origins of the dispute until they find themselves in mediation. When stereotyping occurs, parties may believe that a person cannot be trusted because he or she is an out-group member. It is not uncommon to discover that attribution bias led to the dispute or escalated it unnecessarily.

One's in-group is comprised of individuals who share certain identity traits, such as religion, social class, geographic origin, race, ethnicity, marital status, gender, political affiliation, or occupation. In other words, an out-group is comprised of individuals who share few identity traits or with whom one's in-group has had historic conflicts. In expecting future bad behavior based on attribution biases and stereotyping, parties can create unfounded mistrust.

Misunderstanding of Mediation

Parties to mediation often misunderstand the process itself, the role of the mediator, and the extent to which agreements are binding and enforceable. A lack of understanding about the mediation process can lead parties to exhibit distrust. It can also lead them to assume that the other side will find ways to use the mediation process as a tool to hurt them further or stall an unfavorable outcome.

There are two basic misunderstandings of mediation that can interact with mistrust between parties and thus lower the willingness to participate. One fear might be that information shared in mediation could be misused. Parties can be afraid to share information out of distrust for how the other party might use it. Mediator Julie Barnes explains that "[parties] don't know if information may be used against them if they go to trial." Another fear might be related to the low confidence in implementation of the agreement. As mediator Jerome A. Diekemper says "[Parties] don't know if there are default provisions that can be added to the agreement."

STRATEGIES FOR BUILDING TRUST

As discussed previously, parties usually come to mediation with a trust deficit. Expert mediators use a number of tools to address the challenges of mistrust between parties. These tools range from explaining mediation to building procedural trust in the process. When parties trust the process, they are reassured of the confidentiality of the information shared, the safeguards to assure compliance and enforcement of agreements, and can be confident that despite mistrust, a satisfying solution might be possible and worth working towards.

Focus on Finding a Solution

Mediators from our panel of experts stated that they sometimes prefer to focus on finding a solution to the problem as opposed to addressing the relationship between the parties. Focusing on finding a solution is not a strategy to avoid the issue of mistrust, but rather a means of moving forward.

The assumption being that when things start to move forward, mistrust will be less of an issue.

How Mediators Focus on Finding a Solution

Expert mediators help parties focus on the solution rather than the mistrust in several ways. One strategy is to help parties focus on how to make the future better instead of concentrating on the past. Rather than keeping the parties focused on their bad relationships, they begin brainstorming options for changes or settlements that might meet their needs. Mediator Evan Ash says, "[I would] have each party describe what they would like the outcome to be and what they are willing to do to get there."

A second strategy would be to conduct a cost/benefit analysis with the parties. Specifically, they are asked to weigh the benefits of settling the case now versus costs of prolonging the dispute, including the emotional toll, the time spent, and the financial costs. Mediator Tony Newport explains, "I do a conflict costing process in which I ask both parties to assess the pros and cons of resolving a conflict now or resolving it later." Often, both parties have incentives to reduce the transaction costs of a lengthy conflict.

Another strategy would be to help parties realize that their positions are not as far apart as they believe. As mediator Maartje Van-der-Vlies, states "[I would] have them discuss what they want and show them how much they do have in common." Focusing on commonalities helps to build identity-based trust while searching for solutions that meet the substantive needs of all parties.

When Focusing on Finding a Solution is Appropriate

Expert mediators like to have parties focus on finding a solution when parties enter mediation anticipating bad behavior or ulterior motives. This may mean reframing the problem. Mediator Julie Barnes' story illustrates the use of this strategy:

> In a landlord/tenant dispute, the tenant wanted to keep a dog that the landlord was complaining about. The tenant got upset because he thought the landlord was telling him he had to get rid of the dog or move out. After I determined that the landlord did want to keep the tenant, and the tenant wanted to stay in the property, I helped the parties get to the real issues with the dog and found that the landlord was not saying that the dog had to go, only that the tenant had to keep the premises free of the mess created by the dog. They were then able to reach an agreement.

When parties are afraid of being taken advantage of, expert mediators use this strategy to help parties move forward. The idea is to focus on positive anticipations rather than negative ones. Mediator Douglas E. Noll explains the use of this strategy,

> I asked the distrusting partner in an on-going business dispute what was important about accountability and what he would need to feel safe. We worked on very specific objectives, standards, and behaviors with a detailed dispute resolution agreement. They designated me as their neutral and I have never heard from them.

Risks of Focusing on Finding a Solution

Staying focused on finding a solution is a low to moderately risky strategy. This is most useful when the trust concerns and past breaches were relatively minor, and when trust is built during the mediation process so that it is no longer an obstacle to settlement. The main risk with this strategy is that by focusing on the solution, the mediator may be ignoring the underlying concerns about distrust. If trust is a serious issue and the mediator refuses to acknowledge the party's concerns, he or she risks alienating one or both sides.

EXPLAIN THE MEDIATION PROCESS

One recurring mediation strategy used to compensate mistrust between parties is to explain the mediation process. Once parties understand they are not giving up their right to have a judge hear their case, or other administrative remedies, then they may be willing to give it a try. The premise of this strategy is that if parties can trust the mediation process, they can participate even if they do not trust each other. Thus, procedural trust in mediation can compensate for a lack of relational trust between the parties.

How Mediators Explain the Mediation Process

Usually, parties need assurances that they will not be coerced into reaching agreements and that their concerns will receive full consideration during the mediation process. The first strategy is to explain to parties that mediation is a risk-free process because there is no obligation to settle. Mediator Julie Barnes says, "I tell them that they do not have to settle or agree to anything if they do not want to, but that many cases do settle, and ask them just to give it a try. That is almost always successful."

It is also helpful to explain the enforceable nature of agreements resulting from mediation. Many parties are unaware that mediated agreements can generally be enforced by courts as applicable to the type of dispute. As a result, another strategy is to explain how a mediated agreement is binding and can be enforced. Mediator Sally Lord says, "The benefits of a legally enforceable agreement are explained to all parties, as well as the option of a Parenting Plan. The value to children is that they have a predictable, enforceable regimen, and therefore a more secure environment."

When Explaining the Mediation Process is Appropriate

Obviously, explaining the mediation process works best when one or both parties doesn't know that mediation can address their concerns. This is especially true when one party does not trust that the other party will implement the agreement. In such cases, explaining how mediation works can remove barriers related to mistrust. This strategy is illustrated by Julie Barnes,

> In a landlord/tenant dispute, the landlord does not want to make an agreement because 'what if he doesn't pay or move out on time as agreed?' I show them that the court has a provision for a judgment or writ of possession upon default of the tenant. Also, I can point out that the court gives out orders and judgments, not checks.

Risks of Explaining the Mediation Process

Explaining the mediation process is a low-risk strategy and parties generally view it as a fundamental duty of the mediator. Once parties understand they have little to lose by trying mediation, that agreements are enforceable, and that everyone will have a chance to be fully heard, they usually see the ways in which mediation can be of assistance even if they mistrust each other. However, sometimes explaining the mediation process is not enough and mediators have to use additional strategies such as those proposed in this chapter.

BRIDGING TALKS BETWEEN PARTIES

In some cases, disputants are willing to try mediation, but only if they do not have to directly interact with the other party. They may wish to have mediation done through the use of caucus-based meetings with no joint sessions. In other instances, parties are willing to meet, but the lack of trust means they need the mediator to establish ground rules that allow them to feel there is a safe space where their needs will be heard and they will not be mistreated or disrespected by the other party.

How Mediators Bridge Talks between Parties

In some cases, parties are so distrustful or their levels of anxiety and apprehension are so high, they prefer to mediate without ever seeing the other party. In such cases, the mediator's strategy is to use shuttle diplomacy. As mediator Sally Lord puts it, "The concerned party would be offered the opportunity for telephone mediation or shuttle mediation where they would never have to physically confront the other party. It is then up to the mediator to build confidence in them and in the process." In fact, technology can be used in many ways to enable parties to mediate without ever being face-to-face (Conley Tyler and Raines 2006). From teleconferences, to e-mail mediations, online meeting services platforms, Skype, and other technologies, if parties want to mediate at a distance, they certainly can do so. This can be especially important when bringing the parties together poses a safety threat, such as criminal cases or divorces with domestic violence.

Another strategy is to reinforce mediation rules to make parties more comfortable to deal with each other. Creating a safe space for the sharing of information can be done by mediating at a distance, through caucus sessions, or joint sessions. One way to facilitate this is to create and enforce ground rules the parties feel are adequately protective and meet their needs for emotional security and respect. Mediator Rachel Fishman Green shares a story to illustrate this point:

> The husband said he was reluctant to share thoughts because they would be ridiculed. I explained that he might feel more comfortable in another process—maybe mediation isn't right, if he is not able to share these thoughts—but we could not continue without his input. I then asked him how we could create a safe space—e.g., [his] wife would promise not to react at the moment, but give him some time to process his thoughts and make sure he is heard and understood. She agreed to hold back reaction (write it down) and then he said what he was thinking.

A third strategy is to encourage sharing perspectives before exploring the issues. Expert mediators get parties to share information and perspectives, with the hope they will come to see each other in a different light. In effect, they seek to humanize the parties in each other's eyes. In such cases, expert mediators will facilitate productive and civil information sharing. By encouraging information sharing and by ferrying this information as needed between the parties, the mediator acts as a bridge as he or she helps rebuild trust. According to mediator Don Greenstein,

> [My] goal is to help the parties to see each other in a new light. I meet with them jointly and separately, asking open ended queries with the intention of helping them share information that might illustrate they can trust each other. Then it's my job to point this out and ask them to share this insight/information with the other parties in the next joint session.

Finally, a useful strategy is to depersonalize ideas to help parties focus on the message and not on the messenger. Mistrust leads parties to automatically reject ideas coming from the other side. This is a psychological bias known as reactive devaluation, that makes it difficult for individuals to objectively assess proposals or offers coming from an adversary (Ross and Stillinger 1991). The same offer made by anyone else would be more attractive than the offer from one's adversary. Mediator Steven J. Gold gives us an example of this strategy, "For ideas or proposals that appear to be mutually beneficial, and if there are some from both sides, I may incorporate some from each side in a comprehensive mediator's proposal for them to consider. This removes a certain amount of the identification of the proposal as coming from one or the other side."

When Bridging Talks is Appropriate

Expert mediators use various strategies to bridge talks when parties assume bad motives or anticipate bad behavior from the other party. By bridging talks, the mediator helps parties feel safe to express their opinions. Usually, mediators will use a combination of strategies to bridge talks between parties. Here is a story from an expert mediator to illustrate this point:

> The divorce mediation was proceeding in caucus due to mom's hostility towards dad. Dad wanted slightly more than 2 weekends per month, but mom said his only goal was to seek a reduction in child support to account for the increased parenting time. Mom said that dad was a workaholic and his absenteeism had led to the divorce and his weak relationship with his three teenagers. In caucus with dad, he broke down sobbing. He said the divorce led to an epiphany and he needed to change his life if he was to have any deep relationship with his kids. He had already asked his boss to allow him to work 4, 10-hour days so he could have Fridays off to go to his kids' sporting events, take them to school, and pick them up afterward. He wanted to spend time with them before it was too late and they were out of the house. He wasn't seeking a reduction in child support for this extra parenting time. It became clear to me that he needed to share his feelings directly with mom. We reconvened in joint session and there were tears all around before it was over. Mom consented to dad's request for more parenting time. It was a moment that reminded me why I love this job.

Risks of Bridging Talks between Parties

Acting as a bridge between the parties has a low to moderate level of risk involved. The major risk of bridging talks is hindering the power of face-to-face communication. When there is a low level of trust between disputants, they often feel more comfortable allowing the mediator to speak for them or conducting the mediation session in ways that avoid direct contact. However, this greater level of comfort can come at a cost to the goal of repairing relationships. When parties communicate directly and face-to-face, they can look into the other's eyes and size up his sincerity or lack thereof. If a party is truly remorseful for his past actions, an apology conveyed via the mediator will not carry the same weight as one delivered directly.

BUILDING TRUST IN AGREEMENTS

When the parties already have significant knowledge of one another due to frequent negative and disappointing interactions in the workplace, community, or home, then it can be difficult to rebuild relational trust in the time allotted for mediation. In these cases, it makes sense to focus on procedural trust (i.e., trust in the process and outcome). With procedural trust, the parties can be trusted to abide by their agreements because the incentives for doing so are written into the agreement itself. For procedural trust to work, the certainty of the penalty's enforcement must be clear to all.

How Mediators Build Trust in Agreements

Several strategies can be used to build trust in agreements. A first strategy used by expert mediators is to plan a mechanism to monitor the implementation of the agreement. An expert mediator gives an example: "I ask what could be done to provide some assurance, one to the other. One option that emerges is a future maintenance meeting, which requires only one party to call for it. I find that it is useful to discuss trust and the permanency of loss of trust." Parties may have more faith that each side will abide by the agreement when they know there will be a neutral third party available to arbitrate, mediate, or simply witness violations of that agreement.

A second strategy is to include penalties that will occur if any provisions of the agreement are not fulfilled. This is an example of calculus-based trust, which is founded on knowledge of existing sanctions, such as rewards or penalties (calculus-based trust). With calculus-based trust, individuals can be trusted because it is in their interest to behave as contracted or expected (Lewicki and Bunker, 1995).

As mediator Steven J. Gold explains, "Usually there is a way to incorporate satisfactory repercussions/penalties in the case of noncompliance. This also helps test the sincerity and ability to comply." Such agreements, therefore, need to be very explicit and specific as to the duties of each party, including detailed timelines. Applicable laws may limit the penalties that parties can include in agreements. For example, the amount of financial penalties for late rent might be specified in local landlord/tenant laws and mediated agreements cannot exceed those amounts.

In money matters, this might mean payments are deducted from paychecks automatically or sent in certified mail so there can be no doubt as to whether or not the check is in the mail. For a domestic relations case, this might include supervised visitation for a defined period of time or drug/alcohol screening to verify sobriety. As for juvenile cases, it could include references to expectations for verifiable school attendance, grades, or community service. Mediator Jerome A. Diekemper gives some examples of penalties: "When compliance with an agreement is really an issue, I suggest building some enforcement mechanism into the agreement, such as liquidated damages, attorney fees to the prevailing party, and/or a consent judgment that allows a party to seek a contempt citation from a court in the event of a breach."

Furthermore, theories of procedural justice predict that individuals are likely to have the highest compliance with provisions they recommend themselves. Many of our mediators stressed the inherent value in allowing parties to be creative in coming up with their own provisions related to compliance verification and penalties for noncompliance. Mediator Julie Barnes uses this principle when she "ask[s] [parties] what remedy they would like to have if a provision of the agreement is not fulfilled. If they do not know, I can help them think of some, or let them know of some that are in place, depending on the setting."

A final strategy used by expert mediators is contingent agreements. Sometimes the future is uncertain and each party may have a different prediction for the future or for the future behavior of the other party. In this type of situation, it can be helpful to create contingent agreements based upon the differing predictions of the parties as to what the future holds. These agreements tend to take this type of format: If *X* happens by (insert date), then we both agree to do *Y*. If *X* does not happen by this date, then we agree to do *Z* instead. Contingent agreements allow both parties to react to changing future circumstances without needing to renegotiate the contract or come back to mediation if one party fails to uphold his promises. Here is an example of a contigent agreement from mediator Maartje Van-der-Vlies:

> Two brothers were arguing over their parents' estate and one of them had received a great deal of money on several occasions to help him restart his life, but each time he had wasted it on drugs. The brothers agreed that the addicted brother would go into rehabilitation and they agreed that if he went back on to drugs in the next two years then he would give up his claim to the estate.

When Building Trust in Agreements is Appropriate

Expert mediators must build trust in the agreements when one party is afraid that the other will use mediation to gain an advantage, have no intention to comply with the agreement, or is just trying to buy time. Mediator Jerome A. Diekemper's story illustrates this strategy:

> In a recent non-compete case, the employee breached the employment contract, but was then able to secure non-breaching employment (i.e., employment that abides by the previous non-compete contract). The employer did not trust that the employee would not go right back to employment in breach of the non-compete contact as soon as the agreement was signed, dismissing the case with prejudice (which means it cannot be filed again). I suggested the parties enter into a consent decree where the employer could seek an immediate contempt citation in the event of a breach (a consent decree is an agreement in which one party admits no fault but agrees to specific actions or a financial settlement). I felt the employee was sincere about wanting to maintain the non-breaching employment, and she showed that by agreeing to the consent decree.

When parties have a history of breached interpersonal trust, using procedural trust is a strategy that is often used by expert mediators. Procedural trust can be created with very specific provisions. Mediator Douglas E. Noll gives us an example of how this strategy was used to help a father and son move toward an agreement:

> A father and son own a business and are in deep conflict. The son feels betrayed by the father. We negotiated a trust and respect agreement that specified expectations, behaviors, and accountability when there were violations. The father and son stuck by the agreement and repaired their relationship in 6 months.

In other cases, procedural trust will be built by using legal provisions in the agreement. Obviously, this strategy will be used in cases of severe mistrust between parties. Jerry Wood relates:

> In a landlord/tenant case, a tenant agreed to pay one half of the back rent by a certain day and the remainder in equal, weekly installments. The landlord had no confidence that the tenant would live up to the terms of the agreement and [thought he] would have to start the eviction process all over again. The parties agreed that the tenant would pay up front the court costs already incurred, that a writ of immediate possession would be issued without delay, but would not be executed as long as timely payments were made.

Risks of Building Trust in the Agreement

The use of procedural trust in agreements is a relatively low to medium risk strategy. In fact, parties usually ask mediators to include provisions for penalties or contingencies for noncompliance. The main risk is that a party who is not absolutely sure he will comply with the terms of the agreement may walk away from the table rather than sign it. In this case, the parties have been saved the drama of crafting an agreement that will likely not be fulfilled. While it may result in a slightly lower settlement rate, the settlements achieved will be more sustainable and legitimate.

However, mediators need to take a balanced approach when it is time to integrate legal provisions, in case the agreement is not implemented. For instance, the fearful party may ask for too stringent provisions and thus scare away the other party. Regardless of the underlying reasons for the mistrust between the parties, it is important for the mediator to refrain from appearing judgmental or partial toward either party. Building trust in the agreement is a way for the mediator to help the parties reach an agreement in spite of distrust, but it is best if the specific provisions originate from the parties themselves, so as to avoid the appearance of mediator bias. For the cases in which the mediator suggests terms based on calculus-based trust, it will be important for both sides to understand that the mediator's motivations for doing so relate only to his legitimate interest in helping the parties find an agreement that works for them both. If the mediator's suggestions appear to come down too hard on one side, then this strategy becomes riskier.

SUMMARY

Parties come to mediation after something has gone wrong with a transaction or a relationship. Often these problems have eroded the trust between parties, making them hesitant to participate in mediation, share information, and reach agreements. Past experiences between the parties often lead them to be concerned about whether agreements will be fulfilled or respect will be shown. Mistrust due to past problems often poses serious challenges for the mediation process, including a history of being disappointed, fears of being taken advantage of, anticipating bad behavior from the other side(s), and a general misunderstanding of the mediation process which hampers progress and leads to impasse. Expert mediators suggest a number of strategies to address the challenges posed by mistrust in the mediation process, including the need to focus on finding a solution, explain mediation, act as a bridge or buffer between wary parties, and build trust in agreements. Table 3.1 summarizes strategies used by mediators to deal with mistrust between parties.

Table 3.1. Summary of Strategies to Deal with Mistrust between Parties

STRATEGIES	HOW?	WHEN?	RISK?
Focus on Finding a Solution	*- Look forward - Cost/benefit analysis - Minimize gap between positions*	*- Anticipated bad behaviors - Fear of being taken advantage of*	*- Alienate parties - Underlying issues are not being addressed*
Explain the Mediation Process	*- Risk-free process - Binding and enforceable agreement*	*- Misunderstanding of the mediation process*	*- Insufficient motivation*
Bridge Talks between Parties	*- Shuttle diplomacy - Set discussion rules - Facilitate information sharing - Depersonalize ideas*	*- Anticipated bad behaviors*	*- Do not harness the power of face-to-face interaction*
Build Trust in Agreements	*- Monitoring agreement implementation - Legal provisions in case of a breach in the agreement - Contingent agreement*	*- Fear of being taken advantage of - History of disappointments*	*- One party may be scared off by the severity of the provisions*

Chapter Four

Dealing with Difficult Attorneys

But I don't have an attorney with me. Can't you tell me what this all means and what I should do?

I always tell my clients not to settle in mediation. We'll win at trial. Why should we settle?!

My client has nothing to add. I will do all the speaking for my client in this mediation.

The mediators in our study had a plethora of reasons why they find it challenging to work with attorneys in mediation. First, attorneys might choose an adversarial approach in mediation. In such cases, joint gains become difficult. In other cases, attorneys will not allow their parties to speak for themselves, even though research has shown this strategy reduces parties' satisfaction with their attorneys and with the process itself. Reconciliation between parties may be hindered by a lack of direct communication between them. In some cases, only one side is represented by legal counsel. Mediators then struggle to maintain the power balance while remaining impartial. Finally, in rare cases, an attorney's interests may be somewhat different from those of his client. Sometimes, a mediation impasse might be the best outcome in the attorney's mind!

However, working without attorneys in mediation may be almost as hard as working with them. Therein lies the conundrum. While the rules for dealing with pro se parties differ across mediation programs, parties without attorneys frequently need legal advice, opinions on the strength of their cases, and strong reality checks that would be inappropriate for the mediator to offer while maintaining the appearance of neutrality. Attorneys can also help emotional clients calm down and feel more comfortable dealing with the other party. In fact, an attorney can be a valuable resource in mediation, and most are. Recent research by Poitras, Stimec, and Roberge (2008) has found that the presence of an attorney in mediation does not significantly lower the probability of reaching a settlement.

For some scholars, it is not the presence of an attorney in mediation that matters; it is the attorney's performance that will determine whether his or her presence was a destructive or constructive force. For example, Spier (1999, 22) argues, "The outcome of a mediation session depends, to a large degree, on the performance of counsel." However, putting all the responsibility for a mediation outcome on an attorney's performance would be unfair. Mediators need to work effectively with attorneys as well. Learning to work with attorneys may be challenging, but it is a requirement for becoming a successful mediator.

WHY IS DEALING WITH ATTORNEYS A CHALLENGE?

Dealing with attorneys is not just a challenge faced by novice mediators; this challenge was also noted by the expert mediators in our study. One of the root causes of this challenge might be the traditional curriculum in law schools. As Mori Irvine points out (2003, 45): "Unfortunately, our adversarial system has produced many attorneys who are ill-equipped for the mediation arena. Because of their lack of preparedness or antipathy to anything other than litigation, some lawyers actually impede the settlement process."

More specifically, we asked our panel of experts why dealing with attorneys might be challenging. Their answers can be broken down into roughly five categories: competitive and adversarial approaches by attorneys, misunderstanding of mediation, the presence of only one attorney, attorneys who want to speak for their clients', and, on some occasions, conflicts of interest between an attorney and his client (see Figure 4.1).

Attorneys Who Take a Competitive/Adversarial Approach

Attorneys who take an adversarial or competitive approach to mediation create obstacles to settlement and interest-based negotiation, thereby causing major challenges for mediators. According to our pool of expert mediators, attorneys take an adversarial approach for various reasons.

Sometimes, they might be trying to show off for their clients. As mediator Daniel E. Gulden pointed out: "[Some attorneys] may also feel that they need to show a regular opponent they can be tough and will go to the mat." Attorneys may also want to be in control of the mediation process to show their client that they play an important role in the process. Mediator Douglas

Figure 4.1. Mind map of reasons why dealing with attorneys might be a challenge

E. Noll noted that, "Lawyers want to be in control and are afraid of what their clients will say." At other times, they may be compensating for a weak party or case. They may also feel threatened by the mediator. But the main reason attorneys take a competitive approach may simply be that they have highly competitive personalities, mindsets, or training. Mediator G. Michael Smith states "Sometimes the lawyers get caught up in the battle. Rather than putting their swords away, they keep brandishing them."

Unfortunately, most law schools train litigators rather than preparing negotiators and problem-solvers. These skills must then be learned on the job, often in the mediation room. Attorneys who maintain an adversarial approach in mediation are likely to unnecessarily draw out the dispute, thereby increasing their clients' costs and decreasing satisfaction with the attorneys' performances. It can be particularly difficult when attorneys blur the lines between representing their parties and personalizing the dispute, nearly becoming a party themselves, as pointed out by mediator Chris Carlsten:

> I had attorneys who simply wouldn't stop throwing barbs at each other and the other's clients. I pulled one side into caucus and simply didn't get them together again with the clients present. The attorneys met, then the clients asked to meet without the attorneys and settled the case on their own.

Attorneys Who Misunderstand Mediation

When attorneys do not understand the mediation process and its benefits, they often behave in ways that create obstacles to settlement. As mediator Alexander Yaroslavsky shares, "Attorneys are sometimes not familiar with the alternate dispute resolution (ADR) process, or are nervous about their ability to look competent in front of their clients or boss or partner." Mediator Daniel E. Gulden adds, "The attorney may not understand the dynamics of mediation and how best to represent the client to achieve resolution." This and other information shared by our mediators indicates that misunderstandings about the mediation process, its dynamics, and the best way to represent clients at mediation, are regular challenges for mediators dealing with attorneys.

Beyond simple misunderstanding, some attorneys actively misuse the mediation process. For example, sometimes attorneys attempt to use the mediation process as a quick and easy way to accomplish the discovery necessary for the litigation process. This means that attorneys come to mediation to learn about the other side's case: what witnesses they will call, whom they will depose, and what evidence they have to support their case or to undermine the other side's case. In fact, some attorneys actually like to come to mediation for this exact reason: they can get a peek at the other side's case and determine what kind of settlement offer, if any, makes sense. To the extent this information furthers their ability to make or accept appropriate settlement offers, these tactics may still benefit the goals of mediation. It is when attorneys extract information with no intention of considering settlement in mediation that this becomes problematic.

Because of this, attorneys may be uncomfortable with coming to mediation because they fear the information shared will be used later in the courtroom. As mediator Don Greenstein said, "Attorneys are fearful about controlling the mediation process or not sharing any smoking guns during a mediation session—they fear the other side will use mediation as a discovery session." Because of the fear of misuse, some attorneys see the information shared in mediation as a negative consequence rather than a positive one.

Only One Attorney is Present

Whether mediation is occurring as a pretrial attempt at settlement, as part of an in-house employment mediation process, or even in a community mediation center, parties are generally allowed to bring legal representatives if they choose to do so. Some will choose to bring an attorney with them, while others will come on their own. As a result, expert mediators deal with attorneys in some cases or at some phase of the dispute's lifecycle.

There are many reasons why parties come to mediation without an attorney and continue pro se, despite a mediator's recommendation to get legal counsel. First, many parties cannot afford an attorney or find one to represent them on a contingency fee basis. Second, some people do not trust attorneys and therefore seek to represent themselves through all phases of a dispute's lifecycle, including mediation. Third, some parties believe that the other side will also be coming to mediation without an attorney and are unhappily surprised to find they were mistaken when they arrive at the mediation session. Last, legal ramifications may not be obvious, and parties may think an attorney is not necessary.

Clients with attorneys will have an easier time navigating the procedural requirements required by courts and agencies such as the U.S. Equal Employment Opportunity Commission (EEOC) or the U.S. Environmental Protection Agency (EPA), both of which regularly use mediation to solve disputes. Furthermore, according to Rosenbloom (2002, 1), "Lost in the world of legal procedure and substantive law, the pro se litigant often finds herself confused and overwhelmed, if not frustrated and bitter." Non-represented parties may be at a disadvantage compared with represented parties, creating a power imbalance.

The main challenge posed when only one party is represented is the potential power imbalance that can occur when one side's attorney seeks to impose his own interpretation of the law on the other party or otherwise introduce a bias into the process. As one of our expert mediators noted:

> In a divorce mediation, only the husband had an attorney present. The wife wanted legal advice from that attorney, and we both explained that the attorney could not offer that. The husband wanted the wife to hear the advice his attorney had given to him. However, I felt that would be too coercive, so I suggested we meet in separate rooms. I helped the wife understand that the attorney had to argue the case for her husband's position, and if she had an attorney that person would not necessarily argue the same point of view. We met in separate rooms for the rest of the mediation."

Attorneys Who Want to Protect their Client/Will Not Let their Client Speak

Another key challenge is when attorneys will not let their client speak. Several reasons may explain this situation. Firstly, sometimes attorneys know their client well enough to know that the client's case has some holes that he does not want revealed to the opposing side. As mediator G. Michael Smith put it, "The lawyer is concerned the client will blow the case by saying something wrong or let out information they are trying to keep out of any court proceedings." This strategy, right or wrong, is used when an attorney believes he knows the case and/or client well enough to recommend the silent partner strategy at the mediation table—where the client sits quietly and only speaks when his own attorney directly asks him a question.

Another reason why attorneys sometimes require a client's silence is lack of preparation. Research into the role of attorneys in mediation leads to the same conclusion: "Despite the growing use of mediation, there is uncertainty on the part of many attorneys concerning how to prepare for a mediation and, equally important, how to prepare their client for mediation. Often, the lack of appropriate preparation and understanding about the process contributes to the failure of the mediation" (Meyerson 2009, 1). This lack of preparation for mediation is a frequent problem that leads attorneys to ask their parties to remain silent in the presence of the other party. As mediator Jerry Diekemper comments, "The attorney sometimes may have not spent enough time preparing their clients to talk and therefore won't let them speak because they do not know what will be said."

Finally, in some cases, it might be that the client does not want to talk because he is timid or feels he does not have the communication skills necessary to successfully plead his case. Some individuals may be uncomfortable with conflict or feel they lack the assertiveness necessary to successfully negotiate for themselves. There are many good reasons why a client prefers to have an attorney speak for him or her. The problem is that often times the attorney speaks for the party out of sheer habit or a misguided belief that it is always in the client's interest to stay silent. This results in missed opportunities for resolution, greater understanding, and real closure.

Why is it problematic for the attorney to do all the talking? Isn't that what they are paid to do? Yes and no. Attorneys are most helpful in mediation if they provide legal advice to their client, weigh in on the strength of their case and the other side's case, and provide advice about what settlement offers to make or accept. Attorneys are also helpful when it comes to filing the necessary paperwork; they also know how to respond to interrogatories and other procedural or informational requirements that occur in the litigation process.

Studies of mediation indicate that a big part of the magic of the mediation process stems from the ability of the parties to tell their own stories. For example, complainants who brought attorneys with them to the United States Postal Service (USPS) employment mediations were significantly less satisfied than those who brought no representative with them (Bingham, Kim, and Raines 2002, 371). While various explanations for this exist, the strongest explanation is that parties are allowed to speak for themselves and tell their own story when they come to mediation without a representative. When an attorney is doing all the talking for his client, he kills the magic of the mediation process and leaves his client feeling bereft of the opportunity to tell his own story in his own words—a key factor in procedural justice.

In the courtroom, only arguments about legal rights are allowed. In mediation, parties can talk about the impact the conflict has had on them, including the emotional and nonfinancial impacts, in greater depth than they can in court. They can ask for an apology, seek reconciliation, or mend a business or social relationship. They can vent if necessary. When a party leaves mediation, she should feel like the mediator and the other party really heard what she had to say. This deeper understanding of each party's needs is often what makes a voluntary agreement possible. Mediator Ericka Gray provides this useful example:

> In a case involving an employee who was disciplined for having brought her dog to work, the attorney was doing all the talking. I asked, 'What kind of dog is it?' The attorney responded, 'I don't know,' and looked at the client whose eyes lit up. Out came the photo of the dog and we spent the next few minutes sharing photos of all our dogs . . . even the attorney's dogs! The mediation progressed in a much more informal and productive manner from there.

Conflict of Interest

Most attorneys put the needs and desires of their clients first, even if that means settling a case in mediation instead of taking the case to trial and incurring many more billable hours. Most attorneys are good at separating the legal and emotional aspects of a case for their client, explaining why a client's anger or need for revenge is not a good basis for a lawsuit. Yet the mediators in our study noted that the interests of the attorney, on rare occasion, take priority over the needs of their clients.

In negotiation literature, this is called the principle-agent problem and is the subject of much research. The principal is the party and the agent is the person representing the party. For example, when buying a house, the principal is the buyer and the agent is the realtor. Of course, the realtor gets paid on commission, and therefore has an incentive to see the house sell for a higher price than the buyer might want to pay. Therefore, the agent's interests are not fully aligned with the interests of the principal in the negotiation. In the case of mediation, the agent is the attorney. One expert mediator relates an example that may help to illustrate those instances in which an attorney's interest may be quite different from that of the party he represents:

> I had an absolutely terrible divorce case with domestic violence issues. The husband had shot the family dogs on videotape and sent [the videotape] to his wife, he sent a rifle shell in the mail to the wife, and had done all manner of scary things. The judge issued a protective order and temporarily suspended his parental rights. He had two lawyers on his team, one a senior partner and one a junior partner in the firm. The senior partner popped into mediation halfway through and told dad that he would definitely get full custody of his kids at trial and that the lawyers could get the protective order removed so he could see his wife and kids during the divorce process. On his way out the door, after dangerously inflating the dad's expectations for the case, the junior partner

> whispered to the senior partner that the dad's retainer check to the firm had bounced. Then the senior partner told the junior partner to settle it today in mediation as he walked out the door. Needless to say, the case did not settle. Shortly thereafter the junior partner left the firm to join the opposing counsel's firm in this mediation. She told me that she had to get away from the *Dark Side*.

Because mediators are not allowed to interfere with the relationship between the party and his or her legal counsel, a situation similar to the one described above can be a dicey situation. Mediators cannot advise parties to ignore their attorney's advice, tell them to seek a second legal opinion, or separate the client from his/her attorney. To do so would be unethical and professionally dangerous. Moreover, mediators have disincentives to anger or oppose attorneys in their cases, since attorneys are often repeat customers of a mediator's services. On many mediator rosters, it is the attorneys who recommend a specific mediator to their client. Navigating the ethics of the relationships between mediators and attorneys can indeed be critical to a mediator's livelihood and reputation. Although a conflict of interest is not the most frequent challenge, it is often one of the hardest to overcome in mediation.

STRATEGIES FOR DEALING WITH ATTORNEYS

Our mediators have shared a number of strategies for dealing successfully with attorneys in mediation. While dealing with difficult attorneys becomes easier with experience, expert mediators stress the importance of learning this skill in order to become successful. Expert mediators use several strategies to overcome the challenges of a difficult attorney. These include discussing the best role for attorneys in mediation, using caucus, naming the problem, talking about how the current strategy isn't working, talking directly to the party instead of the attorney, and attempting to balance power when only one party is represented.

Discuss the Best Role for the Attorneys

The strategy most frequently used by expert mediators is discussing the attorneys' role with the attorneys, and sometimes with the parties, during the first mediation session. What is the best role for attorneys in mediation? Ideally, attorneys provide explanations of relevant laws and legal procedures to their clients. They can tell their clients what would most likely happen if the case were to go to court. Attorneys help parties separate legal issues from emotional issues in a case. They encourage parties to maintain realistic expectations of the value of the case and offer a more objective opinion of their clients' levels of liability or responsibility for the dispute. Attorneys can provide information about the costs of unnecessarily prolonging a dispute. When attorneys play these roles, their presence in mediation serves the goal of dispute resolution and enhances the experience of their parties. Yet some attorneys treat mediation as if it were an adversarial rather than collaborative process. This reflects an incomplete understanding of the mediation process and their role within it.

How Expert Mediators Discuss the Role of Attorneys

Many of the mediators told us they speak with attorneys prior to mediation to help them prepare for their roles. Mediator Don Greenstein explains, "[I] talk to the attorney before mediation occurs and share with them how an attorney can effectively help their clients advocate in a mediation session. I share how I work and ask if they can share this with their clients before the mediation." Remember, most law schools do not require courses in mediation, let alone strategies for representing clients in mediation. These are skill sets that most attorneys gain through trial and error rather than preparatory training.

Other mediators talk about the role of attorneys within the first mediation session instead of or in addition to the premediation groundwork. Sometimes mediators ask attorneys to play a different role in mediation than they are used to in litigation. Mediator Jerry Diekemper shares an example of this strategy: "In my opening remarks in joint session, I tell the parties that I expect the attorneys to take off their *advocate hats* they wear in joint session and to put on their advisor hats in the caucus sessions. Then, if necessary, I remind them of which hat they are supposed to be wearing."

Sometimes mediators resort to having a caucus with the attorney(s) during the mediation in order to further explain why attorneys need to change their strategies or adversarial stances in mediation. In such meetings, mediators generally attempt to explain to attorneys why mediation requires a collaborative, problem-solving approach rather than a competitive or adversarial approach. Sharing information about procedural justice concerns and participant satisfaction can also be helpful in convincing attorneys that their clients are likely to be more satisfied with an attorney who approaches mediation different than litigation. Mediator Don Greenstein shares an example of this strategy:

> Having talked to attorneys before the process, when an attorney does not listen and wants to control the process, I'd take a break and talk to them separately with or without their client and explain it again. I ask them to allow their client to talk and they can fill in the blanks. If they refuse, then I explain that mediation may not be the best tool for their case.

When Discussing the Role of Attorneys is Appropriate

Explaining mediation and the role of attorneys in the mediation process is particularly useful when the challenge involved in dealing with attorneys arises from a misunderstanding of mediation. Some attorneys are open to feedback and experimentation with their roles, displaying a willingness to try different approaches and find what works best with a particular client or case. As mediator Chris Carlsten states, "I have found that most attorneys are amenable and cooperative."

Nevertheless, other attorneys may seem to be *one-note Charlies*, unable to vary their bulldog negotiation tactics. In such cases, attorneys might be unable or unwilling to vary their approaches based on the circumstances they face. Once it is clear that the attorney is not open to trying a collaborative approach in mediation, mediators may have to use other strategies to deal with attorneys rather than simply explaining the benefits of a non-adversarial approach. An expert mediator illustrates this point:

> On rare occasions, I have ignored the attorney and spoken directly with the party. I have asked attorneys to give their clients an estimate of the additional legal fees that will be incurred if the case goes all the way to a trial. Sometimes I play dumb and ask the attorney to explain to me why and how he chose his current strategies, in caucus of course. The attorney will usually admit that this is the way he always does it. Then I ask whether it might make more sense to tailor his selection of strategies to the needs of the particular case, and then we brainstorm all the ways to move forward. In the end, if the attorney is simply not willing to engage in interest-based negotiation, then I suggest that perhaps mediation is not the right process for them.

Risks of Discussing the Role of Attorneys

There is little risk associated with discussing the role of attorneys in mediation. However, not all attorneys are open to feedback from the mediator about their roles in a case. The major risk would be to hurt the attorney's ego. Therefore, mediators should frame their observations and suggestions tactfully in order to make it clear that, in the end, it is the attorney and his party who will decide how best to negotiate or proceed with their case. It is wise to highlight that attorneys will play a key role in the decision making while stressing the proper role of attorneys in mediation. The best attorneys to have in mediation are those who allow their clients to tell their own stories, who provide frank advice about the fairness of any settlement offers, and who share information on the likely costs and benefits of settling in mediation versus proceeding with litigation.

Use Caucus

Using caucus to conduct shuttle mediation is another common strategy expert mediators use to deal with difficult attorneys. The main objective of this strategy is to control communication or, more specifically, limit the impact of attorneys on the mediation. Caucus allows mediators to have greater control over the process. In addition, caucus gives mediators a better chance to get information about the parties' interests.

How Expert Mediators Use Caucus

Sometimes, mediators transition to caucus when they are dealing with a particularly adversarial attorney. In such cases, caucus is used to explore options without the presence of the other party's attorney in order to reduce the hostile posturing that often occurs when this attorney wants to signal that his client is unwilling to compromise. An expert mediator illustrates this strategy:

> A husband had an affair and spent a large amount of marital funds carrying on the affair. The wife's attorney could not let it go, and was quite sharp about accusing the husband, requiring proof that every current expense was a marital expense, saying he had to take the bulk of the debt, et cetera. I suggested that we go to separate meeting rooms, and then I was able to discuss the settlement in more realistic terms.

In addition to exploring options without posturing, using caucus can be helpful to find out why attorneys are taking an adversarial approach. In this example, from mediator Jerry Wood, getting the attorney needed information helped change his strategy and make his presence useful instead of destructive:

> An unprepared attorney took an overly competitive style of negotiation in mediation. Of course, the opposing counsel assumed a competitive style as well. In caucus the attorney stated that he did not have enough information to properly evaluate the case. I asked what he needed and was able to procure documentation from the other side. The attorney changed from a competitive negotiation strategy to a strategy of compromise and the case was resolved.

When Using Caucus is Appropriate

When it is used to short-circuit difficult attorneys or gain a broader understanding of attorneys' posturing, using caucus is a stand-alone strategy. However, in most cases, resorting to caucus simply paves the way for other strategies, rather than being a strategy in and of itself. Caucus can be combined with an effort to educate the attorney about the benefits of a non-adversarial approach, or it can be used to separate a pro se party from an attorney on the other side who seeks to provide one-sided information or otherwise create a power imbalance. Mediator Ericka Gray shares an example of this strategy:

> In a particularly contentious divorce case, the wife hired an extremely adversarial attorney who appeared to make it his mission to derail every agreement that the parties had arrived at in mediation sessions. The husband, although extremely difficult in mediation sessions, had hired a very collaborative attorney who was working hard to achieve a reasonable agreement. I ended up meeting with just the attorneys to deal with the issue of derailing the parties' agreements.

Risks of Using Caucus

In general, using caucus in mediation is a low-risk strategy. However, depending on the country you are in, it might be inappropriate to separate a person from his or her attorney. In these jurisdictions, mediators cannot evict attorneys from the mediation process, and it is always ethically complicated to do so. As a result, mediators occasionally find it helpful to caucus with difficult attorneys in the absence of their clients. This allows mediators to dig a little deeper into why the attorney is pursuing an adversarial strategy without fearing any loss of face in front of the client.

The major risk of using caucus is that interactions are restricted between parties and thus the potential for reconciliation is limited. It is difficult to build relationships or authentic understanding between individuals who do not communicate directly. Seeing the regret, fear, or angst on the other's face may help the party recognize sincerity, build trust, and rehumanize the other party in his or her mind. When an *Aha!* moment happens and the other side is not there to see it, an opportunity for building understanding between parties has been missed.

Name or State the Problem

Another favorite strategy of expert mediators is stating how the presence of a difficult attorney may hinder the mediation process. The core of stating the problem as a strategy involves the mediator being explicit about what he or she is seeing: the ways in which the attorney has become an obstacle to productive negotiations. Why does stating the problem work? Sometimes parties get so focused on their positions that they no longer notice the mounting transaction costs. Parties may also fail to realize that their attorney's behaviors might add unnecessary obstacles to settlement or increase the cost of settlement. Mediators should also keep in mind that sometimes the problem may be that an attorney is unaware that he is hindering the mediation process.

How Expert Mediators Name or State the Problem

The problem can be stated in a straightforward way or indirectly. Expert mediators recommend first being subtle. Sometimes though, the mediator explicitly states what he may perceive as a conflict of interest. However, most of the time, the mediator will note that the attorney is not fully hearing what her own client has said, and then ask questions to further uncover any principal-agent problems. As mediator Jerry Diekemper points out, "Most lawyers respect what is in the client's best interest. On rare occasions, I have spoken to attorneys in private to suggest that they listen to what I hear their clients saying about their desire to settle and avoid risks."

When attorneys' behaviors are incompatible with mediation, expert mediators will also state the problem as a strategy to break the impasse. The mediator may point out that mediation is different from court and ask the attorney if she could alter her approach to be consistent with the different venue. The mediator may choose to ask the attorney more about his or her own concerns or worries about the use of mediation for the case at hand, in order to understand where the unproductive behavior is coming from. Mediator Ericka Gray explains her strategy: "[I] discuss with the lawyer and client how the behavior is affecting the mediation. Sometimes I meet with just the attorneys if posturing is involved."

Any of the state the problem approaches can be done in joint session or caucus, although caucus is likely the venue of choice since there is an inherent risk of loss of face for the attorney whose behavior is identified as causing problems in the mediation.

When Naming or Stating the Problem is Appropriate

Naming the problem is mostly used when the mediator feels that there might be a conflict of interest between the party and her attorney, or when an attorney's adversarial stance is making settlement negotiations difficult. Mediators do not want to invoke this strategy too early, since it may alienate the attorney and place the blame for impasse on the attorney rather than on the legitimate differences between the parties' interests and positions. Mediator Jerry Wood illustrates this strategy,

> In an estate dispute, the parties were so involved in an argument about what Mom would want, that they had not considered how many attorneys' fees were accumulating. When I asked how much attorneys' fees would be coming out of the estate, the parties were surprised at how much had already accumulated. Settlement was reached during that session.

Most mediators try to make progress even when faced with difficult attorneys and only name the problem once it is clear that an attorney's uncooperative or counterproductive behavior is becoming an overwhelming obstacle to settlement. Cases can and do settle even when one or more attorneys are difficult to work with. However, when the attorney becomes the primary obstacle to settlement, most mediators will seek to address the problem, usually in caucus.

Risks of Naming or Stating the Problem

Stating the problem can be a high-risk strategy, especially when the mediator is highlighting a principal-agent problem: it can be akin to questioning the attorney's motives and ethics. When a mediator makes a statement regarding the obstacles created by the behavior of difficult attorneys, he or she runs the risk of angering the attorney, especially if the mediator was correct in his or her observation. Using a private caucus with just the attorney may be a softer way to approach the problem. Stating the problem may alienate the attorneys present, but highly ethical attorneys are generally willing to have an honest discussion with their clients about the costs and benefits of their services or their approach to the case. If an attorney is truly pursuing her own interest at the expense of her client, then there is no way to get around the fact that pointing out this behavior will likely alienate or anger the attorney. Here is an example from an expert mediator:

> One time, a party in mediation realized that his own attorney was the obstacle to settlement in the divorce. The husband repeatedly said that he did not want to "go for the jugular" even though his wife had been unfaithful, but the attorney was determined to get a punitive property settlement. First, the husband asked if I would mediate between himself and his attorney. I said that I was uncomfortable doing that and then he fired the attorney. After a brief break, we continued and reached a full settlement.

Talk Directly to the Party

Expert mediators told us they used the strategy of talking directly to the parties in mediation in cases in which the attorney is taking over. By encouraging the parties to tell their own stories, the mediators are likely to get a richer, more complex view of the situation rather than hearing about the legal merits only. Even if the attorney launches into the opening statement on behalf of his client, the mediator can turn to the client and ask if she has anything to add.

How Expert Mediators Talk Directly to the Party

Expert mediators use a variety of strategies to talk directly to the parties, thus avoiding conversations being too filtered by the attorneys. A first strategy would be to simply explain to both parties and attorneys that, in mediation, parties can and should express their concerns directly. For example, mediator Daniel E. Gulden states, "I explain that mediation allows them to have their say as they could not in a courtroom and to have some control over the outcome. After the attorney has spoken, I encourage the party to add anything to the extent he or she is comfortable and with the attorney's permission—rarely denied." Instead of soliciting parties' input in joint sessions, other mediators prefer to solicit parties' input in caucus. Mediator Jerry Wood gives an example: "In caucus, I will note that the client has said very little and will emphasize that their participation is welcome."

A second strategy would be to ask parties to validate attorneys' input. As mediator Daniel E. Gulden says, "You can't make the client talk against the wishes of the attorney if the client wants to trust the attorney. One can ask the client if he or she has anything to add, with the attorney's permission and to the extent they feel comfortable." Moreover, there are times when the party wants their attorney to speak for them, and this is their right. Nevertheless, asking parties to validate what their attorneys say can still be used, as this example from mediator Jerry Wood illustrates:

> A prominent domestic relations attorney routinely tells his client, "Let me do the talking." It is also obvious that the attorney coaches his clients to let him do all the talking in mediation. On one occasion, I turned to the client and said, "I know your lawyer is doing all the talking, but do you understand everything?" and "Is there anything you would like to add?" Eventually, the client said, "You are so kind to ask, but my lawyer has said everything I wanted to say and said it very well."

Third, the mediator talks directly to the parties, usually by asking personal questions that offer little risk to the party's position, consequently indirectly involves the parties. Mediator Lorig Charkoudian gives an interesting example: "I ask participants a question about their day-to-day experiences or their personal experiences in the situation that the attorneys can't answer." Another expert mediator reported, "I ask the parties to tell me the names and birthdates of their children. While the attorney flips through the paperwork looking feverishly for this information, I turn to Dad or Mom and jokingly say 'C'mon, you can tell me.' This usually gets them to join in and realize there is a lot their attorney doesn't know about them and their family."

Finally, the mediator can simply ask a party's attorney for permission to talk directly to his client. One expert mediator described this strategy as, "I ask the attorney for permission to speak directly to the client. I always start off this effort with a question about what the dispute has meant to them or how it has impacted them personally. Attorneys understand the benefit of this information, but are not able to really give it." This strategy works best in caucus because, if the other side is not present, attorneys are generally much less concerned that their client will say something that weakens the case.

Mediators must keep caucus conversations confidential, so using a caucus to get the parties to speak is an extremely low-risk strategy for both the attorney and the mediator.

When Talking Directly to the Parties is Appropriate

Talking directly to parties is the preferred strategy when attorneys are doing all the talking. Timing is important. However, asking parties to speak up too quickly can be a problem. In fact, some parties prefer that their attorneys do the talking. They might be overwhelmed by the conflict, intimidated by the other party, uncomfortable with their own ability to participate fully or early, or they might simply prefer taking the back seat. For these reasons, it is often recommended to let the attorney fully explain the case first before talking directly to the client. One expert mediator gave us an example:

> In a mediation between the guardian of a 4-year-old child and the mother of that child, the mother's lawyer did all the talking. Looking at the mother, it was clear that she was intimidated by the presence of the guardian, his lawyer, a guardian ad litem appointed by the court, and her lawyer. So I let the lawyer speak for her, then the guardian spoke, the guardian's lawyer, and finally the guardian ad litem. I then summarized the issues and asked everyone if I had listed them correctly and completely. At that point the mother spoke up with another issue. I feel certain that if I had insisted she speak at the beginning, she would have resisted and it would have taken her a lot longer to talk.

Risks of Talking Directly to the Parties

The risk associated with speaking directly to the parties depends on the nature of the questions asked. Talking directly to the client is less risky when the question asked is related to the party's personal experience of the conflict or his emotional reactions to what has happened. These are questions the attorneys cannot readily answer, nor do they deal directly with legal matters. It may be a riskier strategy for a mediator to ask a party whether she wants to accept an offer of settlement or ask the party to make a settlement offer. Anytime an attorney feels that his role has been usurped, his strategy is being undermined, or that his client's case is being negatively impacted, then he is likely to react negatively to the mediator's attempts to draw out his clients. Using caucus might mitigate these risks. The caucus can include only the attorney or can also include the party, since ultimately, it is the party's decision as to which strategies to pursue in mediation.

Balancing Power

When one party is pro se and the other is represented, expert mediators use a number of important strategies for balancing power. In truth, rather than balancing power, these strategies are more correctly thought of as limiting the impact of power imbalances. There may always be power asymmetry between a manager and an employee or between a landlord and a tenant. Parties may have power imbalances due to differences in educational levels, communication skills, or even personalities that are easier or harder to work with. Mediators cannot level the playing field by siding with the underdog or by pressuring either side to capitulate. Instead, mediators can remind all parties they have the right to legal counsel, they can terminate the process without an agreement, and they can request a caucus if they feel they would be more comfortable or feel less pressure in the absence of the other party and his or her legal team. In caucus, mediators can give a party more time to think through proposals or help a party work on her framing of the problem in order to respond more effectively to the other party. Mediators can help nervous parties by normalizing their feelings so they become more at ease.

How Expert Mediators Balance Power

The mediators in our study use a variety of methods for addressing the power imbalances that can occur when only some parties bring attorneys with them. These strategies include: reminding the unrepresented party that he or she has the right to counsel and do not need to sign anything before getting legal advice; asking the unrepresented party if he or she understands everything as it happens; providing necessary explanations or information as appropriate; and using caucus to separate the represented and unrepresented parties. Mediator John Settle illustrates how he combines these strategies to balance power in mediation:

> I will let the non-represented party know during my intro that they have the right to consult an attorney etc. I want both sides to hear that. I usually will, subtly at most, try to provide a little more attention to the unrepresented party just to balance the table a little. I may give the unrepresented party a little extra time in caucus, and I may try to translate or repeat statements and offers from the attorney to make sure the unrepresented party is really hearing everything. If I think the attorney is taking advantage, I will, if necessary, stop the mediation until and unless the unrepresented party gets counsel.

When a mediator provides legal information to parties, some mediators ask the party's attorney permission to avoid looking like they are taking sides or they do it in caucus. As mediator G. Michael Smith explains, "I have on occasion asked the lawyer who is present if I may inform the pro se party about a matter or if I can give them some limited and clearly agreed upon suggestions or advice. Most of the time, the lawyer is truly grateful for this suggestion." Sometimes this missing information is what is keeping the client from settling the case in mediation.

When Balancing Power is Appropriate

Power balancing strategies are mostly used when one party is represented and the other is not. Before balancing power by giving legal information, mediators should check rules that would apply to the mediation process. Rules about this vary by jurisdiction and country. Some mediators are allowed to provide legal information, but cannot tell clients what they should do or how to interpret that information in their case. Mediator Ericka Gray notes, "Informed decision making is key and, if parties do not have the information that they want, I will provide the time for them to get it or, when appropriate, provide the information."

Should a mediator decide to balance power by providing information, she should do it as early as possible in the mediation process for two reasons. First, it is important to keep the power imbalance from intensifying. Uninformed decisions can add up quickly and it may become hard for the mediator to rectify the situation later in the process without appearing biased. Second, it is better to start giving information when the stakes are low, such as at the beginning of the mediation session. It may be easier for the other party's attorney to accept a mediator's input when the information provided to the unrepresented party has a low impact on the negotiation's outcome. Providing information that would tilt the outcome at the last minute would likely be perceived as biased.

Note that sometimes a party's attorney can be helpful to the other side. An attorney may provide definitions for legal terms or concepts in a way that is fair and neutral. An attorney may encourage both sides to speak directly to one another and only chime in when called upon for legal advice or information. An attorney may provide balanced assessments of the time or money necessary to take the case to court or discuss the benefits of settling in mediation. Mediator Alexander Yaroslavsky tells this story that illustrates how an attorney can be helpful to both parties:

> In a community dispute resolution center, one side showed up with an attorney. The pro se party didn't mind, so I invited everyone into the mediation room. In my introduction, I stated that I view the attorney in the room as a person who may help the parties to reach a settlement. That framing prompted the attorney to speak up, often to help me by explaining the legal side of a proposal. Toward the end of the mediation, the attorney actually pressed his own client to be more reasonable and offer an accommodation to the pro se person. As we were getting ready to resolve the case, I advised the pro se party that it was his choice to not sign the agreement until he had his attorney review it.

Risks of Balancing Power

Some of the strategies for balancing power are low-risk. The use of caucus and reminding parties of their right to seek legal counsel are generally common, low-risk strategies. Giving more time or attention to the underrepresented party is moderately risky: if it becomes obvious, either party could take this as a sign of bias. Providing legal information or advice to a party has variable risk, depending on the rules of the mediation program or jurisdiction. In some, this is forbidden, while in others it is routine. When providing information, mediators need to be careful to frame it as neutrally as possible so as to avoid the perception of bias.

A riskier strategy is asking the attorney in the room to provide legal information or interpretations for both sides. Some attorneys will use this as an opportunity to present definitions, terms, case law, et cetera, in a way that promotes their client's position. In the interest of settlement, some attorneys are willing to define common legal terms or discuss similar case rulings within the jurisdiction. Others will use this as an opportunity to promote their client's case. Before turning to this strategy, the mediator needs to follow his or her intuition as to whether the attorney will be able to present information in a neutral fashion. If this backfires, then the mediator may need to break to caucus in order to repair the damage.

SUMMARY

Dealing with attorneys in mediation can be challenging for many reasons: competitive and adversarial approaches by attorneys; misunderstandings of the mediation process; the power imbalance when only one attorney is present; attorneys who want to speak for their clients; and, on some occasions, conflicts of interest between an attorney and his client. Successful mediators have developed numerous techniques to deal with the challenges of having attorneys involved in mediation. These include discussing the best role for attorneys in mediation, using caucus, naming the problem or talking about how the current strategy is not working, talking directly to the party instead of the attorney, and attempting to balance power when only one party is represented. Table 4.1 below summarizes how experienced mediators deal with attorneys in mediation.

Table 4.1. Summary of Strategies to Deal with Difficult Attorneys

STRATEGIES	HOW?	WHEN?	RISK?
Discuss the Best Role for the Attorney	*- Explain mediation in pre-mediation* *- Explain mediation in first joint session* *- Explain mediation during caucus*	*- Misunderstanding of mediation*	*- Hurt the ego of the attorney*
Use Caucus	*- Explore options in private* *- Probe reasons for adversarial approach*	*- Competitive attorneys*	*- Limit the potential for reconciliation*
Name or State the Problem	*- Name in front of both attorney and party* *- Name only in front of attorney*	*- Conflict of interest* *- Competitive attorneys*	*- Alienate attorneys* *- Attorneys quit mediation*
Talk Directly to Party	*- Solicit input from parties* *- Ask parties to validate what their attorneys said* *- Involve parties indirectly* *- Ask permission to talk directly to parties*	*- Attorney wants to talk for client*	*- Alienate attorneys who feel bypassed*
Balance Power	*- Remind parties of their rights* *- Verify whether parties understand everything* *- Provide necessary basic explanations*	*- Only one attorney present*	*- Being perceived as biased*

Chapter Five

Dealing with Cultural Differences

She is so hypocritical, she doesn't even look at me when she talks!

He can't just promote his relatives instead of qualified applicants!

He can't dress like that and be taken seriously at work!

At first, these positions may appear to have nothing to do with cultural differences. Upon closer inspection, you might find these positions to be built upon cultural assumptions that are held by some, but not all, of the parties to the conflict. Gender role expectations, acceptance or nonacceptance of hierarchy and authority, belief in the utility or inappropriateness of nepotism, and even the definition of "punctual" are all culturally embedded concepts that give rise to misunderstandings and eventually impasse when they are not adequately explored in the mediation session.

Intercultural differences refer to the wide range of communication problems that naturally appear when individuals from different religious, linguistic, social, ethnic, and educational backgrounds. It is likely that cultural differences pose an even greater challenge than its ranking indicates because this challenge is so frequently misidentified and labeled as something else, such as intransigence, close-mindedness, a lack of understanding about the mediation process, or the old standby communication problems (Avruch 2003).

As the use of mediation increases, mediators are more likely to be involved in cross-cultural mediation. Even the most skilled and experienced mediator will face new challenges in cross-cultural mediation. The mediators in our study found that cultural differences posed increasing challenges during the mediation process. An expert mediator puts it this way, "As with power differences, cultural differences exist in most disputes. So I go in with the idea that cultural differences are what they are. They are always there, so let's get on with it."

Experienced, successful mediators have found ways of dealing with cultural challenges in order to help parties progress, solve problems, and reach resolutions. This chapter will examine the reasons why cultural differences may create a challenge for mediators. Then we will examine strategies used to overcome intercultural challenges, and share mediator success stories.

WHY CULTURAL DIFFERENCES MIGHT POSE A CHALLENGE

We asked mediators to be specific about the reasons culture may pose a challenge to mediators and parties. A story from an expert mediator helps illustrate how cultural bias can be tricky:

> In a recent workplace dispute, a supervisor was of Balkan origin and the underling was a sort of Californian flower girl. She felt bullied and had made a charge. The supervisor had a stern exterior and looked a bit like one of the war criminals on trial in Croatia. His English was not bad, but without the nuances (of course). As the exercise proceeded, it became clear that he was the one in the greater emotional pain and that he was the one who needed to heal. It would have been easy to make a culturally-oriented assumption.

According to our panel of expert mediators, language differences were not at all the primary source of intercultural misunderstandings in mediation. While language challenges do create difficulties, it is really the deeper cultural differences that are the hardest to overcome. Our panel of mediators gave us four main cultural challenges: belief and custom, ethnocentrism, language, and expectations about outcome (see Figure 5.1).

Beliefs and Customs

Expert mediators stated that differences in beliefs and customs posed the greatest culturally-based challenges to resolution. As mediator Steven J. Gold points out, "Cultural differences may cause differing perspectives more than miscommunication or misunderstanding." In addition to beliefs and customs surrounding the dispute resolution process and what neutral means, many differences are likely to exist around the dispute itself. Our culture tells us how to behave in specific circumstances: what is appropriate to say or not to say, who is responsible when something goes wrong, which problems are small enough to let go and which should be pursued. As mediator John E. Sands states, "Culture provides context. And well-established cultural norms are in their bones and can't be compromised."

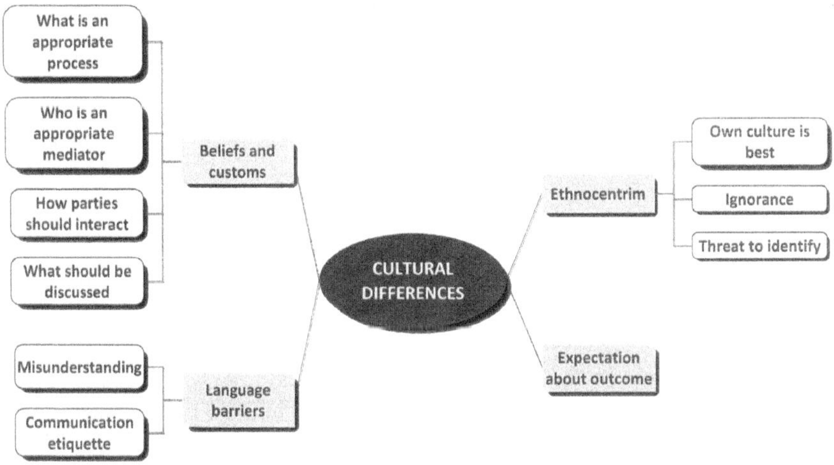

Figure 5.1. Mind map of reasons why cultural differences may pose a challenge

Cultural beliefs and customs are the first type of challenge to the mediation process. Parties may have differing views about the value of their case that are culturally based; they may also have culturally-influenced perspectives on right, wrong, fair, etc. Differing cultural beliefs may lead one party to believe that mediation is an appropriate process, while the other party feels that it is inappropriate to share such personal information with a stranger. For example, in many Arab cultures, the mediator is a trusted community leader who knows both families and is respected by all sides (Pely 2010). A stranger's advice would be inappropriate.

A second challenge may be attitudes towards the mediator himself. A party may feel that negotiating on a matter of moral right and wrong jeopardizes their very soul by requiring them to compromise their identity-related beliefs (Benjamin 1998). Cultural beliefs may impact perceptions about who should serve as a mediator and who should not: gender, age, sexual orientation, nationality, race, and religious affiliation or lack thereof, could influence whether a mediator is deemed an appropriate choice (Charkoudian and Wayne 2010). Disputants may feel that only someone from their own culture can fully understand the conflict or the positions of the parties. Parties may believe that the problem itself is not a matter for the courts (i.e., culturally based beliefs about what is private versus public), or that one party's power or status means that she should be treated differently than the other.

Additionally, customs may dictate how parties and the mediator should relate to one another. Differences in customs may lead to inadvertent insults or perceived rudeness between parties and/or the mediator, getting mediation off to a poor start. For example, in some cultures, men do not shake hands with women. If a man refused to shake the hand of a female mediator, she may take this personally, thereby making it difficult to remain neutral and impartial during the mediation process. Caucus would also be used differently in some cultures. In cultures where saving face is critical, mediators may rely more heavily on caucus, where each party can speak more frankly without causing embarrassment to the other party (Ogawa 1999; Volkema 1988).

Finally, culturally based knowledge may come into play when determining what should be considered acceptable evidence or where the burden of proof lies. In criminal matters, some cultures require the accused to prove his innocence, while in other cultures the burden of proof is on the accuser. Different cultures also handle issues such as pain and suffering differently. In the United States, there are likely fewer restrictions on how much a plaintiff can be awarded for pain and suffering than there are in most other Western countries. Expectations around the role of insurance in claim payouts may be highly varied among disputants from different cultures as well. All of these beliefs and customs surrounding dispute resolution processes and the neutral role of the mediator can lead to challenges pertaining to legitimacy, trust, and shared understanding within mediation.

Ethnocentrism

Our panel of expert mediators pointed to ethnocentrism as a root cause of many cultural challenges in mediation. Intercultural communication scholars define ethnocentrism as viewing one's own ethnic group as the norm, with all other ethnic groups are judged in reference to one's own cultural norms and expectations (Neuliep 2009). Ethnocentric groups and individuals see their own group's worldviews and norms as universally correct and superior to those of others. As mediator Maartje Van-der-Vlies notes, "They assume their culture is the dominant one with rights."

Ignorance of the cultural norms of the parties can cause misunderstandings on the part of the mediator and the parties themselves. Even well-intentioned parties and mediators are often unaware of the cultural roots of a particular dispute or behavior. As mediator Sally Lord points out, "We live in a very culturally diverse society but do not have intimate knowledge of all cultures." The more one is exposed to other cultural groups, the clearer it becomes that there are multiple interpretations of right behaviors in specific situations.

Moreover, it frequently remains difficult for one party to acknowledge the alternative behaviors as equally right as one's own. Identity theory states that anything that may challenge someone's identity will be met with fierce resistance (Haslam 2004). As mediator Bruce Engelbert notes, "A party's identity can be so rooted in their culture they are unable to accept what the other party needs."

Language

Expert mediators also mentioned language barriers as posing a challenge in mediation. As one expert mediator reports, "Language difficulties and different cultural expectations can quickly make small matters into disputes." To make matters worse, not all concepts can be translated easily. As mediator Bruce Engelbert explains, "Some linguistic and cultural concepts don't have equivalent translations in another language or culture." Thus, language can create challenges in mediation in different ways.

Firstly, language can create misunderstanding or trigger strong negative emotions. Both verbal and nonverbal communication can create challenges in intercultural mediations, especially when trying to communicate in a foreign language. One of our expert mediators shared this illustrative anecdote: "In a sexual harassment case, one party kept saying the mediator should *feel up* the other party, when he meant *feel out* the other party." These small differences can fan existing flames of distrust in cases in which parties come from groups that are historically at odds or when parties are already distrustful of one another. In addition, rules for making or avoiding eye contact vary by culture. This nonverbal form of communicating respect can cause serious misunderstandings that give rise to conflict both outside and inside mediation.

Secondly, language barriers can also take the form of differences in communication etiquette. For example, in U.S. mediation trainings, mediators typically spend significant time practicing their listening skills. They are taught not to interrupt parties or speak over them, except as necessary to enforce ground rules. To interrupt or speak over a party is considered quite rude and unprofessional. Yet the norms and skills for listening are different in Chinese culture, where people who agree with one another commonly speak over each other with no hard feelings or perceptions of rudeness resulting. Even the pitch, volume, and pace of speech vary between linguistic and cultural groups. What sounds like yelling to someone from Culture A may sound normal to someone from Culture B.

Expectations about Outcomes

Sometimes a party seems to hold an entrenched position out of sheer stubbornness when, in fact, their position can be traced to their assumptions about the strength of their case in the justice system with which they are familiar. As mediator Don Greenstein says, "People have set ideas of what a normal settlement may entail based on the justice system or other widely known and acceptable practices in the local community." The challenge is that these norms are only normal or widely known within one's cultural group, not across groups.

As a result, disputants carry their beliefs about reasonable and customary punishments with them, even when those norms do not fit in well with the local culture. Differences about the expected outcome can create a situation in which one party may ask for major compensation, based on what an offense means in his culture, while the other may expect minor compensation based on his cultural norms.

In one state or country, the penalty for an infraction may be relatively minor, while in another state or country the same infraction may result in a vastly harsher penalty. For example, being caught with a given amount of marijuana in California might result in a small fine, while in Idaho it might result in a five-year prison sentence. Failure to pay child support in one county might not result in any jail time, while another jurisdiction consistently sentences *deadbeat parents* to jail time as well as financial penalties. These differences amount to local knowledge based on the norms of the dominant local community groups (at least in democratic societies).

STRATEGIES FOR DEALING WITH CULTURAL DIFFERENCES

Culture is increasingly playing a role in mediation and expert mediators use a number of tools to address the challenge of cultural differences. These tools range from clarifying what is being said to grounding mediation in fact and law. Along the way, expert mediators also ask to be educated about cultures to better understand how the mediation process should be adapted. When culture is ignored, impasses are likely. However, when incorporated into the mediation process, exploring cultural differences can be quite enlightening about the conflict and open the door to unsuspected agreements.

Ask to be Educated

The most common strategy for dealing with culture-based challenges is to ask to be educated. This means that mediators seek to make implicit cultural assumptions and understandings explicit. It is important to understand what the differences are to better adapt the mediation process. One common mistake is to assume we know these cultural differences. Such assumptions can lead to tragic mistakes. For expert mediators, the basic principle is not to assume knowledge of the differences, but ask the parties to explain these differences.

How Mediators Ask to be Educated

A number of mediators said they would often feign ignorance of a particular cultural norm or expectation so that one party could directly explain their understanding or expectation to the other party. Mediator Don Greenstein recommends allowing the parties to share their cultural perspectives: "I ask questions that bring the differences to the forefront and frequently allow the parties to teach me about the cultural differences (even if I am aware of them)." A variant of this strategy is to ask both parties to educate the mediator. That way, both parties are involved and both feel they have the attention of their mediator. Mediator John E. Sands illustrates this strategy: "When it becomes clear that something is holding up the progress, I engage the parties in a joint effort to identity the problem and educate me (and each other) as to what's going on."

Sometimes, mediators will ask more specific questions about the mediation process or other issues that relate directly to how people interact. Mediation processes differ across cultures and vary by mediation program or jurisdiction. When mediators encounter reticence to participate in mediation or obvious discomfort on the part of one or more parties, it can be helpful to seek input about culturally-based preferences that might be accommodated within the mediation process. In such cases, mediator Douglas E. Noll will ask: "How does your culture ask people to respond in these situations?"

When Asking to be Educated is Appropriate

Asking to be educated is mediators' preferred strategy when they feel that differences in beliefs and customs may create misunderstanding or impasses, especially when the differences lie in dispute resolution customs. Mediator Douglas E. Noll relates a story that illustrates how useful this strategy can be:

> In one mediation, I was working with a Hmong mother and son. The mother did not speak good English and we used an interpreter. She was obviously confused by the process, so I asked her how this type of conflict would have been handled back in her village in Laos. She explained a perfect mediation process. I asked if everyone was OK if we followed that process. Everyone agreed and we conducted a Hmong mediation. It worked great.

Usually, the mediator will ask to be educated in front of the other party to make sure everybody understands why the other acts in a specific way. The goal is to prevent attributions and misconceptions about the other behavior, especially when these attributions or misconceptions are the source of the conflict. Mediator Don Greenstein shares how educating each other about cultural differences can be a turning point in mediation:

> I had a community-based mediation where an Asian shopkeeper was accusing a Hispanic individual of shoplifting from the store. It turns out that the Hispanic person had shopped there on a regular basis for a long period of time. They never conversed, and the Hispanic man wanted some form of recognition of his loyalty to shopping in this store. The Asian shopkeeper shared with me in a caucus that in his culture if he looked the person in the eye he was taking them

> into his family, so he could not do this with every customer. I asked him to share this in the mediation process with the other party. The Hispanic shared in his separate session that he needed recognition from the other party for his loyalty to the community-based store. They both shared openly in the joint session and the outcome was they have been best friends more than 20 years.

Expert mediators also recommend asking to be educated when ethnocentrism may play a role in the mediation process. This might be especially important when it is the mediator himself who is working in a different cultural environment. Mediator Douglass E. Noll illustrates this strategy:

> [I] had to face this in a mediation where I was the only person that could hear. Everyone else was deaf. I learned a great deal about the deaf culture and its conflict avoidant, passive-aggressive norms by asking questions and becoming an active learner.

Risks of Asking to be Educated

Asking to be educated is a relatively low-risk strategy. However, the mediator should avoid looking too complaisant to avoid being perceived as taking sides. There may be a natural inclination for parties to perceive bias toward or against them depending on whether or not they share an identity-trait with the mediator. An expert mediator gives an example: "A man walked into his divorce mediation and immediately said, 'I guess you'll be on her side since you're both women.'" In addition, the mediator should avoid looking patronizing when asking parties to explain the meaning they attach to behaviors or proposals. It is helpful to explain that cultural differences may lead to misunderstandings or misinterpretations and that the mediator is working to rule that out as a possibility before moving forward with other strategies.

Clarify Meanings

Mediators on our panel of experts stated that they regularly seek to clarify meanings through questioning, summarizing, and checking their own and the parties' understanding. Individuals within the same cultural group may reach different conclusions when faced with the same information, but this tendency will be greater as the cultural distance between the parties increases. Rather than competing over which party's perspective is right, it may be helpful to learn more about why a party believes in what she does.

How Mediators Clarify Meanings

Expert mediators rely on several strategies to clarify meaning. The first strategy a mediator can use is to simply ask clarifying questions and paraphrase what the parties are saying. For example, mediator Julie Barnes states, "[I] pay particular attention to making sure that ideas are communicated clearly, by rephrasing if needed, and asking questions to clarify meaning." Sometimes, paraphrasing is not enough and mediators must reframe what is being said. Mediator John E. Sands reports, "I listen intently to everything that's being said and, when I observe a reaction inconsistent with what I've heard, I intervene to translate English to English by reframing the words to express what's intended."

A second strategy a mediator can use is to summarize and validate what is being said by the parties. The objective is to avoid building on false assumptions or misconceptions. Mediator Bruce Engelbert explains, "[I] summarize frequently with simple language and reframing as seems useful. Regularly check in with the parties to determine if they are clear about what is being communicated. I may ask each party to say what he heard from the other."

In some cases, the potential for misunderstanding might be so great that expert mediators will use caucus and shuttle diplomacy to filter communications. Mediator Greg Rooney confirms, "[I use] private sessions to clarify the miscommunications—perhaps some shuttle mediation for a time with the aim of getting back into a joint session as soon as possible." When mediators using caucus have clarified most of the misunderstandings, parties can be brought back together in joint sessions.

When Clarifying Meaning is Appropriate

Clarifying meaning is the preferred strategy of expert mediators when they observe a language barrier between parties or between a party and the mediator. As one expert mediator recalls, "A nonnative English speaker was using an odd turn of phrase that insulted the counterparty, which ran the negotiation off the rails." Clarifying meanings can bring parties a long way toward resolution. Mediator John E. Sands illustrates this point:

> A Japanese businessman kept saying *hai* or yes to what his American adversary was saying. The American became frustrated because, despite each yes, the negotiation wasn't moving. I intervened to explain that, in this case, *yes* meant *I hear you*, not *I agree*. The Japanese fellow immediately changed to *I hear you* instead of *hai*, and we eventually settled.

Risks of Clarifying Meaning

Clarifying meaning is a low-risk strategy. However, mediators should be careful to paraphrase and not restate what the parties said. Mediators should be careful to not induce meaning, as a party may be tempted to agree with what the mediator said without fully understanding what he means. Sometimes a caucus can be used to minimize risk because it may be difficult to ask these basic questions without the risk of making a party feel stupid. For example, a mediator might say, "You mentioned that children always go with the mother at the time of a divorce. Can you tell me why you believe this will happen?" Or an even more basic example: "You said you *beat* your children when they need it. Can you tell me what that *beating* looks like?" In this last example, the mediator might learn that the language barrier results in the use of a term that raises a red flag unnecessarily. Upon further investigation, the mediator may learn that the beating is more correctly labeled a spanking and does not reach the level necessary to trigger intervention.

Ground Mediation in Facts

One important strategy in cases of intercultural management is to clarify local laws and norms in order to help the parties understand how their dispute will likely be handled if it goes forward. Clarifying processes and legal issues is helpful for the party who comes from the minority culture group, as they may have false expectations about what will happen if mediation fails. Moreover, when agreements are reached, it is important to check back with the parties to ensure that they all interpret the meaning of the agreement the same way and fully understand their commitments.

How Mediators Ground Mediation in Facts

Mediators in our sample mentioned that, despite a party's understanding of how a dispute would be handled in their culture of origin, parties should understand that it is the jurisdiction in which they currently reside that will use its own cultural and legal frames of reference to determine the outcome of the case, at least for court-connected mediation. As mediator Steven J. Gold explains, "Cultural issues must give way to the reality of what is likely to happen in the U.S. legal system." Even when laws are similar across jurisdictions, they may be interpreted or enforced differently based on local norms and customs. Getting this local knowledge can be a critical step toward resolution for the parties.

When Grounding Mediation is Appropriate

Grounding mediation in law and norms is the strategy used by expert mediators when parties have culture-based expectations. A mild form of grounding mediation is reminding parties that decision rulings will not be based on culture. Mediator Maartje Van-der-Vlies offers this example, "An Indian and a Baltic state person were determined that they had prime rights, and they were advised that was not the case and their issue had to stand on merit, not culture." A stricter form of grounding would be to explicitly cite laws and norms as a point of reference as to what outcome could be expected. Another example from mediator Maartje Van-der-Vlies illustrates this strategy:

> A Chinese woman and Australian man were business partners and they were arguing about who was to get which share of the business, which was being sold. The Chinese woman was accusing the man of racism to get a big share and this came to a head when a legal definition of racism was given; she changed her mind after three mediation sessions.

Risks of Grounding Mediation in Facts

Grounding mediation in law and fact can be a risky strategy for a couple of reasons. First, many mediation programs prohibit mediators from offering legal advice, and the line between legal information and advice may be somewhat subjective. Many mediators say they will provide a legal definition but then leave it to the parties to decide how that legal term or concept applies (or not) to their case. Second, sometimes one side has a stronger legal case. When the mediator provides legal information, the parties may recognize that one side has a stronger case than the other and blame the messenger. To repeat an earlier example, if a father from the Middle-East is going through a divorce and a custody dispute, the mediator may supply information to indicate there is no gender preference for male custody of children in U.S. family law. As this is bad news for this disputant, he may interpret this as a bias within the legal system or on the part of the mediator. Use of a caucus may help to limit the negative impact of this strategy, as the mediator may seek to soften the blow somehow or allow the party to react to this new information in a private setting.

Clarify Expectations

Expert mediators talk about the need to clarify the parties' expectations. This strategy dovetails nicely with most of the strategies discussed previously. Near the beginning of the mediation, it can be helpful to ask the parties about their goals and expectations for the mediation process and outcome.

How Mediators Clarify Expectations

Clarifying parties' expectations can be very straightforward. An expert mediator puts it simply: "I ask parties about their and the other's cultures, what they expect, and what they expect of me." These simple questions help ensure a mediation process that is useful for all parties as well as clarifying any misunderstanding about the mediator's role early on in the process. It may be helpful to ask them what they expect would happen in court or another decision-making forum. This may reveal a lack of information about local laws or rules, which evolve from the norms of the locally-dominant cultural group.

In multinational organizations, such as the World Bank or Siemens, employees from around the world come together and must craft shared norms that find their way into official policies and procedures. For employees who work together long enough, shared microcultures are created which allow smoother interactions and fewer misunderstandings. Mediators working with multicultural organizations must develop an understanding of the organizational culture as well as the official policies or procedures that will impact the course of mediation and influence the Best Alternatives to Negotiated Agreements (Fisher and Ury 1981).

When Clarifying Expectations is Appropriate

Expert mediators ask parties to clarify their expectations about mediation outcomes when they feel that cultural differences may play a role in what parties hope to achieve in mediation. Sometimes, parties have unrealistic expectations that result in an impasse. Other times, learning those expectations can create a lot of room for negotiation. Mediator Douglas E. Noll recalls a story that highlights this strategy:

> Many Southeast Asian people have strong cultural and spiritual beliefs around nature and the nature kingdom. I have used this as resource to help solve problems without the traditional payment of money. Rites, rituals, ceremonies, and shamanic interventions are all possible tools for mediators in these situations.

Risks of Clarifying Expectations

Clarifying expectations is a low-risk strategy. By asking about how a similar dispute would proceed or resolve in the parties' personal experiences and cultures, mediators can gain valuable insights into why a party will or will not accept a proposal from the other side, as well as understanding the party's alternatives to a negotiated agreement. While most mediation programs do not allow mediators to provide individuals with legal advice, mediators may be able to share basic procedural information or refer parties to external sources.

There are a few risks to using this strategy. First, there may be some loss of face when the mediator admits his lack of cultural knowledge. For most mediators, humility is a job requirement, so this may not pose a significant problem. Second, a party may come to believe the mediator is not the right fit for the case. In fact, this may be an accurate assessment. To ensure the best fit between the mediator and the case, it may be best to find a mediator from the same cultural group as the parties. When the dispute involves parties from multiple cultural groups, co-mediation may be useful to avoid any appearance of bias that may occur when the mediator shares the culture of one party and not the other.

SUMMARY

Cultural differences make for challenging yet fascinating mediations. A mediator's training and knowledge of cross-cultural concepts can allow the mediator to play the role of cultural translator, or at least help him or her identify the root causes of what are often culturally-based misunderstandings. In many instances, these differences have created false impressions, making parties hesitant to participate in mediation and reach agreements. Although language barriers are the first things that come to mind when we talk about cultural differences, our panel of mediators stated that these are not the most challenging aspects of cultural differences. For instance, differences in beliefs and customs can make interactions awkward and unnecessarily inflate conflicts. Ethnocentrism can make parties and mediators from the dominant culture miss important points. Finally, different expectations about what is a fair outcome may hinder negotiation when those cultural differences are not made explicit. Expert mediators suggest a number of strategies to address the challenges posed by cultural differences in the mediation process, including asking to be educated, clarifying what parties mean or expect, and grounding mediation in facts when necessary. Table 5.1 below summarizes strategies used by mediators to deal with cultural differences.

Table 5.1. Summary of Strategies to Deal with Cultural Differences

STRATEGIES	HOW?	WHEN?	RISK?
Ask to be Educated	*- Feign ignorance - Ask about process preferences*	*- Differences in beliefs and customs - Ethnocentrism*	*- Being perceived as taking sides - Being perceived as patronizing*
Clarify Meaning	*- Ask clarifying questions, paraphrase - Summarize and validate - Shuttle diplomacy*	*- Language barriers*	*- Induce meaning*
Ground Mediation in Facts	*- Focus on the problem - State applicable laws*	*- Different expectations about outcome*	*- Being perceived as taking sides*
Clarify Expectations	*- Ask to state expectations*	*- Different expectations about outcome*	*- Being perceived as taking sides*

Chapter Six

Maintaining Neutrality in Mediation

Oh, you're a woman, so I can see where this divorce mediation is headed.

You've worked in management. You know what it is like to deal with these people, right?

I've already told him he is dead wrong. Maybe he needs to hear it from you.

In Western cultures, a founding principle of mediation is the premise that the mediator should be a neutral and impartial third party with no previous relationship to the disputants. While the concept of neutrality is fundamental to the mediation process, it is also contentious and complex. Neutrality is comprised of two composite concepts: impartiality and equidistance (Rifkin 1991; Wing 2009). Impartiality is the ability of the mediator to refrain from bias or taking sides with regard to parties' perspectives or preferred outcomes. Impartiality is defined as "the quality of being principled enough to remain equally committed to the legitimate interests of all parties" (Morris 1997, 321). Equidistance is the idea that a mediator makes symmetrical moves toward each party (Wing 2009, 390), showing sympathy to both, asking difficult questions of both, et cetera.

Neutrality is an ideal that may be impossible to fully achieve. Since neutrality is seen as one of the cornerstones of the mediation process, practitioners have often been reticent to question the centrality of the concept, as well as methods for ensuring or invoking neutrality during mediation sessions. The truth is, some parties are easier to like or dislike. Other times, the mediator may just want to move the process ahead without appearing to take sides. In extreme cases, one party may threaten the role of a mediator, and he may need to assert his leadership without appearing to have a negative bias toward the more challenging party. Some scholars argue that neutrality can in fact recreate or perpetuate societal or organizational inequalities and coercion against lower-power parties (Wing 2009; Li-On 2009). Thus, mediators must sometimes rebalance power between parties to ensure a fair process. In such cases, the mediator may find it challenging to maintain an aura of neutrality.

Neutrality is a mediator quality as well as a set of rather undefined behaviors necessary for a fair process. Janet Rifkin and her colleagues (1991) argue that mediation functions like a folk concept, with a tacit understanding of what it means and how it works, but very little analysis of how the concept works in practice. This is critically important for the benchmarking process undertaken in this book because we have done exactly that: asked expert mediators to explain the strategies they use to maintain neutrality in spite of various challenges that arise during the mediation process.

THE CHALLENGE OF MAINTAINING NEUTRALITY

We asked our panel of expert mediators to tell us more about the challenges of maintaining neutrality and impartiality in mediation. One common thread is that it is often difficult to maintain neutrality even with the best intentions. A humorous story from mediator Steven J. Gold illustrates this point:

> I once had a lengthy joint session to address all of the facts and issues from the respective points of view of each party, reframing as I went along. When we went into caucus, each side expressed that I seemed partial to the other side! That was a bit perplexing. I assured them both that it was my job to try to fully air out all of the facts and issues.

Expert mediators suggest there are a number of situations that give rise to challenges to mediator neutrality. First, it can be difficult to remain neutral when one party is behaving badly. Second, when the parties are stuck and the mediator needs to move them forward or get them off of their positions, keeping an even-handed approach can be tricky. Third, mediators want to ensure a fair process and true impartiality, even in the face of various challenges such as asymmetrical power between the parties. Finally, mediators must be prepared to respond appropriately when a party accuses the mediator of not being neutral or impartial. These challenges to mediator neutrality can be further broken down, as shown in Figure 6.1 and discussed below.

PARTIES OVERWHELMED BY CONFLICT

Sometimes parties can be overwhelmed by the conflict, triggering the mediator's desire to either show empathy or a need to intervene to stop counterproductive behaviors. For example, when people of any age experience high degrees of stress, they may exhibit developmental regression. This means that a person is not acting his age. Developmental regression is most easily spotted in children, such as when their parents are going through a divorce and the household is filled with anxiety or hostility. In this case, a child who had stopped thumb-sucking or bed-wetting may revert to these behaviors inadvertently. For adults in mediation, stress may make a parent act like a teenager or result in highly self-centered behaviors. When parties in mediation are overwhelmed by the conflict, they exhibit fear and anxiety as well as a desire for vindication. These can lead to outbursts or other behaviors that militate against settlement.

As mediator John E. Sands notes, "They're angry. The pain of anger, physical injury, financial loss, and other personal resentments or fears may lock negotiating into punitive or other unproductive agendas that prevent rational valuation of proposals and willingness to put the conflict behind them." Similarly, mediator Tony Newport observes: "Parties are often caught

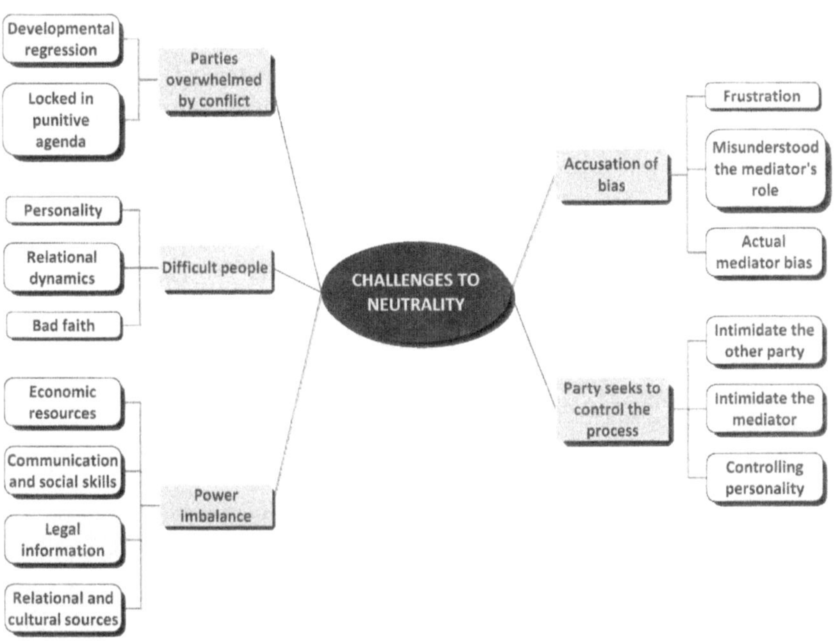

Figure 6.1. Mind map of reasons why maintaining neutrality can be difficult

between wanting to exact some kind of retribution or letting it go and moving on."

In such cases, mediators may feel a need to reach out to them in various ways rather than to treat both sides exactly the same. The mediator may spend more time in caucus with one party in order to help the party regain emotional control or to provide coaching for communication skills or anger management. However, such actions can be interpreted as showing favor to one client over another. Therefore, helping a party deal with the conflict can lead to a perception of bias by the other party. The mediator may seek to explain that this is time well spent in the service of conflict resolution.

DEALING WITH DIFFICULT PEOPLE

Unlike the parties who are overwhelmed by the conflict and who may therefore exhibit difficult behaviors, this group is comprised of people who may be difficult to deal with outside of mediation, even on a good day. Some personalities may make mediation itself more difficult, as some people are overly competitive, argumentative, or defensive. For example, Type A personalities are associated with a high likelihood of verbal aggression in conflict, and thus in mediation (Baron 1989).

In addition, the history of relational dynamics between the parties may require the mediator's intervention to balance power (if possible) or help an intimidated party have a safe space for sharing his concerns. As mediator Maartje Van-der-Vlies notes, "If one party has a history of dominating the other, then the mediator may choose to address this in mediation, leaving one or both disputants concerned about the resulting decline of neutrality." Finally, not all parties come to mediation to attempt to resolve their case. As mediator Bruce Engelbert states, "[Sometimes] one party is stalling or avoiding or not participating in good faith."

In such cases, it is the mediator's role to point to and even label these behaviors if that helps to promote settlement and end destructive behaviors. Yet when a mediator tells a party that she is stalling or appears to be mediating in bad faith, it nearly always impacts the appearance of mediator neutrality. In fact, any strong reality check could lead a participant to perceive a lack of neutrality on the part of the mediator.

POWER IMBALANCE

In his classic work on the mediation process, Christopher Moore (2003) defines power as, "The capacity to influence the outcome for another party depends on the exercise of various means of pressure or persuasion that either discourage or encourage the possibility of various options." Mediators have long debated the need to balance power between parties who have an asymmetrical distribution of power. In reality, mediators cannot make a secretary and a CEO equal in power. Instead, the mediator tries to create a fair process, where all sides are heard and have the ability to share or reject offers for settlement, as they feel best suits their needs. As the mediator strives to ensure a fair process for all, some strategies or techniques used or even the amount of time or attention he gives to each side may vary depending upon the distribution of power and needs of the parties. There is an inherent tension between mediator neutrality and strategies or techniques used to address power imbalances or other needs of the parties (Gerami 2009).

There are many sources of power that parties may or may not bring with them to the mediation. Some parties have economic power, which enables them to bring one or more attorneys to represent their interests and provide legal advice. Communication and social skills may be unevenly distributed between the disputants in mediation. Some are simply more articulate than others. Access to relevant information is another important source of power that is frequently unevenly distributed between the disputants: legal information, information about court or other relevant processes, information about policies and procedures relevant to the conflict, information about the outcome of similar cases in the past, et cetera. Relational power—the power that one has due to their social connections or status—may also be asymmetrically distributed. Cultural sources of power may also be distributed differently. Individuals from the dominant or hegemonic social group will better understand expected behaviors, effective communication methods, when to speak or remain silent, which issues are under the jurisdiction of the court or the mediator, and how to frame their comments more effectively. Finally, general levels of education and cognitive abilities may also be distributed unevenly between the parties, making it more difficult for one or more sides to follow the information shared during the process.

Our panel of mediators mentioned a number of specific types of power imbalance. Mediator Julie Barnes reports, "One party may have an attorney or be an attorney, and the other may not be able to afford representation. One party may be agitated and aggressive verbally, which can be intimidating to some." According to our expert mediators, neutrality challenges are most likely to arise when power differences come from one of these sources: only one side brings legal or other representation to mediation; different levels of information or financial assets; or when one side is physically or emotionally intimidated by the other side, sometimes due to aggressive behavior displayed in mediation. These power differences can result in coercion of parties in mediation, leaving mediators with some difficult choices to make in terms of appropriate techniques and strategies to address these problems.

ACCUSATION OF BIAS

There are various reasons that a party may accuse the mediator of being unfair. Our expert mediators noted that parties may be generally frustrated by a lack of progress or by the mediator's unwillingness to back them up or take their side in the dispute; these can lead to an accusation of bias. Disputants or their attorneys may believe that by attacking the mediator they can gain some strategic advantage or make the mediator overcompensate and treat them better than if no such accusation had been made. For example, mediator Sally Lord says, "Generally, the party making the accusation is not getting their own way. If this person is particularly controlling, they may perceive any discussion which challenges their control over family members as biased." Mediator Bruce Engelbert further illustrates this point with an example: "Something I have said or done may seem biased or unfair to one party. A party may be unhappy with the way the process is headed and try to place responsibility or blame on me."

There may be a perceived lack of neutrality due to a misunderstanding of the mediator's role or the mediation process itself. Disputants frequently do not understand the difference between a judge and a mediator. This is easily detected when the party(ies) argue their case to the mediator, seeking to sway the mediator's opinion of the case and the evidence in their direction. Since control of the case's outcome lies with the parties and not with the mediator, arguing their case to the mediator is counterproductive and indicates a poor understanding of the mediator's role. Yet that misunderstanding can quickly turn into frustration when the party(ies) fail to get affirmation of their perspective or preferred outcome from the mediator. Mediator Don Greenstein explains: "Sometimes a party is frustrated by the process, by the other party, or by my reaction or inaction in not supporting their interest or position."

PARTY SEEKS TO CONTROL THE PROCESS

Occasionally, a party or his attorney seeks to control the process. Parties seek to control the mediation process for a number of reasons: they may be trying to intimidate the other side or the mediator; they may not fully understand the mediation process; they may be impatient with the pace of the process; or they may simply have a controlling personality that leaves them uncomfortable with allowing the mediator to run the meeting. The opinion of mediator Greg Rooney is, "I would say that it is often a strategic move by that party to try and gain some advantage by attacking the mediator."

When a party seeks to control the process rather than the outcome, she is wresting the most important role away from the mediator. It is one thing if a party makes a procedural request of the mediator for strategic reasons (e.g.,

Can we meet in caucus instead of joint session?). It is another thing when the party clearly attempts to assume control of the mediation in ways meant to enhance his power at the expense of the other party or the mediator. An example of this would be an unwillingness to allow the opposition to speak or otherwise dominating the discussion in spite of mediator direction to the contrary.

When a party seeks to control the mediation process, the mediator's attempts to set boundaries could be interpreted as a sign of disfavor against the usurping party or his attorney. Depending upon the circumstances of the situation, the mediator may indeed feel anger or frustration towards the usurping party. Mediators are generally treated with respect and deference, so when one or more parties ignore these expectations, it is likely to raise real and perceived challenges to neutrality at some level.

STRATEGIES FOR MAINTAINING NEUTRALITY

While mediators are expected to remain neutral, the effective fulfillment of their role involves exercising a significant amount of authority and power (Gerami 2009, 433). The trick is to balance the power and authority inherent in the mediator's role with the self-determination of the parties and their ability to control the outcome of their dispute. The more the mediator keeps the power with the parties, the less likely the mediator is to run into allegations of bias.

However, sometimes mediators must intervene in order to maintain an orderly and civil process or to help the process remain constructive rather than destructive. Our expert mediators use a number of tools to intervene in the mediation process while maintaining neutrality. These strategies range from mild intervention, such as reflecting with parties in caucus and explaining the mediator's role and strategies, to stronger intervention, such as naming the problem and stressing ground rules with parties. Talking about parties' expectations is another preferred strategy of our expert mediators.

Explain the Mediator's Role and Strategies

Nearly all experienced mediators have dealt with accusations of bias at one time or another. To address this concern, expert mediators explain the mediator's role and strategies. By maximizing transparency, parties are less likely to worry about a potential misuse of mediator power or feel that the mediator is siding with the opposition. Through an explanation of the mediator's choice of strategies that led to the allegation of bias, it is usually possible to overcome these concerns and move forward with the mediation.

How Mediators Explain their Role and Strategies

The most straightforward way mediators can defuse parties' concerns is to explain their role. For example, mediator Julie Barnes says, "I explain my role clearly, emphasizing that I have no stake in the outcome of their case, remind them it is their case, and they do not have to commit to anything they do not want to do." Alternately, mediators can explain their goals for the mediation. As mediator Rachel Fishman Green explains, "My goal is to put together an agreement which contains no surprises—either when you go to review with attorneys or two years down the road at a cocktail party." Mediators can also be more specific and explain their strategies. Mediator Steven J. Gold says, "I explain what I am doing in reframing/restating and that it is my role not to take sides, but to understand each side, explore the possibilities for resolution based upon where each side is coming from."

Another way to defuse parties' concerns is to ask them to voice their perceptions. The mediator invites parties to share the reasons behind their concerns, either in joint session or in caucus. In a second step, the mediator can answer parties' concerns by asking how he could better meet parties' expectations. Mediator Don Greenstein shares a good example of this strategy:

> I was working with two people in a court-annexed mediation where I felt one party was coming on heavy-handed toward the other party. I had a limited time period before the case had to go back to the courtroom. I pushed the parties jointly for concessions and one of the parties exploded telling me my questioning was biased against her. I broke into separate sessions and asked her to explain her perceptions. She shared that I was asking her more questions than the other party. I asked if I could regain her trust in the process and in my neutrality. She indicated that my neutrality was proven by taking the time to meet with her and acting concerned about the issue.

When parties raise concerns about the mediator's neutrality, mediators should remain open to the possibility that they may have indeed been biased. Some mediators noted the importance of taking time to be introspective and analyze any influences that might reduce their own neutrality. Mediator Don Greenstein also reports, "I explore in a separate session why such perceptions exist and share that my role is to be neutral and impartial. I try to understand where their perceptions come from and look within my own reactions to see if there is something that triggered or blindsided me."

When Explaining the Mediator's Role and Strategies is Appropriate

Explaining the mediator's role and strategies primarily occurs to respond to a party's allegation of unfairness. When accused of displaying bias, mediators should react without defensiveness, explore the concerns that gave rise to the accusation, consider explaining the reasoning behind the mediator's actions or framings, and invite the party to continue with the mediation. Transparency helps parties to trust the mediator and the mediation process. Mediator Rachel Fishman Green offers a good example of how she defuses allegations of unfairness:

> The husband had started a successful business during the marriage, which should be considered as marital property during the negotiations, even if there might not be a payout value to the wife. Neither knew about this. The husband got angry with me, initially, and felt that I was siding with the wife. I reminded him that the goal here is to come up with an agreement that will pass muster and not be unwoven when the wife goes to an attorney to review it. He accepted that and stayed with the process.

A second reason to explain the mediator's role and strategies is to overcome a party's challenge to the mediator's role. When a party tries to usurp control of the process, dominate discussions, violate ground rules, or insist on joint or caucus sessions against the mediator's advice, then she is challenging the mediator's role as the process expert. In these instances, it may be helpful to explain the reasons for the mediator's process preferences to the challenging party. This can be done in joint session or in caucus sessions. Explaining the reasons behind process choices can help show skeptical parties that the mediator's choices reflect both her neutrality and her experience with similar cases. Reminding parties and attorneys that they maintain control over the outcome can help in those instances when a party is simply more comfortable or accustomed to maintaining control.

Finally, mediators may use humor to gain or regain the trust of a party who has voiced concerns about the mediator's neutrality or competence. Mediator John E. Sands gives an example of using humor to defuse a challenge to his expertise:

> A skeptical party challenged me by asking, 'How long have you been doing this?' I replied, 'My first mediation was between my father and my sister at the dinner table. I was six.' She had the grace to laugh and allow me to do my job.

Risks of Explaining the Mediator's Role and Strategies

Explaining the mediator's role is a low-risk strategy. There is little harm to be done in explaining the role and techniques used by mediators and the reasons behind those techniques. Mediators vary in how comfortable they are with revealing their strategies and techniques. If it is in the service of dispute, resolution, and transparency, most mediators do not mind explaining their choice of communication or process strategy. However, some mediators may prefer not to go into detail in these areas out of fear that their intervention will be less efficient. When the mediator explains his choice of strategy, it is akin to looking behind the Wizard of Oz's curtain and revealing the machinery. However, it may be helpful in some cases and build trust in the mediator for parties who are skeptical of mediation's benefits.

Reflect in Caucus

Expert mediators suggested using caucus to help minimize the impact of power differences without raising any concerns about mediator neutrality and equidistance. The use of caucus can help maintain the appearance of neutrality because one party does not see the techniques the mediator uses with the other side. In fact, a mediator could use caucus time to validate one side's claim, perspective, or preferred outcome. The logic is simple: so long as the other side does not see these actions, they are less likely to raise accusations of bias. Of course, one can be accused of bias in favor of a party, just as one can be accused of bias against a party. In the state of Georgia, a mediator was found guilty of a breach of neutrality when he told a divorcing wife, in caucus, that he could understand why she was divorcing her husband. The wife felt that his behavior was both unprofessional and lacked neutrality; even if the lack of neutrality was assumed to work in her favor.

How Mediators Reflect in Caucus

Sometimes, mediators must move a little beyond neutrality to stop a party from intimidating the other one. When this happens the mediator can repeatedly reprimand the aggressor in joint session, thereby appearing to surrender neutrality. She can also resort to the use of caucus so the behavior has no opportunity to continue. Mediator Julie Barnes relates an example of a situation in which caucus was used to stop intimidation:

> A man and his wife were rather loud and insistent. They seemed to think that by being aggressive they could intimidate the other party, a woman. Eventually, I had to caucus because the man and his wife would not relinquish their behavior. I kept the parties in caucus for the remainder of the mediation, until both had the time to think over their options calmly, and they decided to settle.

Another mediator strategy is using caucus as a tool to give the weaker party time to think through options and have a safe space for deliberation. For example, mediator Julie Barnes reports, "I make sure each party has the time and mental space to think through their options. Try not to let either party bulldoze the other." Similarly, mediator Tony Newport states, "Sometimes I remind both parties of what is possible and give them some time to consider. I may make suggestions but they must choose and sometimes they need time."

Mediators also discussed the use of reality checks during caucus to help higher-power parties fully analyze and acknowledge the reasons why they might want to consider settling in mediation, even if they could win in another forum. Mediator Jerome A. Diekemper shares one of his war stories:

> In a court-ordered mediation, the plaintiff was pro se (without counsel) and had a facially valid claim. In private caucuses with the plaintiff, I asked him how he would be able to deal with the daunting tasks of responding to a summary judgment motion and a jury trial with rules of evidence. With the defense, I asked what would happen if the plaintiff survived the summary judgment motion or if the judge appointed counsel for the plaintiff. By getting the parties to focus on what could go wrong in court, they were able to arrive at a non-nuisance value settlement that recognized the realities of their respective situations.

When Reflecting in Caucus is Appropriate

Caucus is the preferred strategy for mediators when they want to balance power between parties. Mediators use caucus time to help lower-power parties in many ways: to isolate them from the pressure or one-sided information they may hear from the other side's attorney when they are *pro se*; to give them time to think through or develop proposals at their own pace; to remind them about their rights to terminate mediation or seek legal advice; help those from a nondominant group to better understand the process and issues in a private setting rather than losing face in joint session.

The use of caucus can help reduce the negative impact of asymmetric power and foster a process in which each party can express themselves at their own pace, in a manner that increases their ability to be frank and collaborative. If it appears the mediator is affirmatively taking power from one side and transferring it to the other, perhaps by sharing information or giving one-sided reality checks, an accusation of bias may arise. The use of caucus results in fewer accusations of bias. Its impact on reducing actual bias is less certain. Mediator Don Greenstein elaborates on this strategy: "[In caucus, I] make certain that both parties share full information and reality check the situation to ascertain that the options are really possible and that one person is not taking advantage of the other party."

Risks of Reflecting in Caucus

The use of caucus is a relatively low-risk strategy that can be used to separate parties with disparate levels of power or to protect a lower-power party from bullying behaviors. This strategy is not risk-free, in that one side may misinterpret the amount of time spent with the other side as a sign of bias or the mediator's greater concern for that party. Alternatively, one side could wonder what the mediator is saying about them in the other's caucus, a concern that does not arise when the mediation proceeds in joint session only.

Mediators can mitigate these risks in a number of ways, most of which require the mediator to be meta-communicative. Mediators need to communicate about how he is communicating. For example, the mediator can explain why one side may require more caucus time than the other: "Please don't read anything into how long it takes me to caucus with one side versus the other. Sometimes it simply takes longer for one side to think through and respond to a proposal or to gather their thoughts." It is also helpful to reiterate that nothing shared in caucus will be disclosed by the mediator unless by agreement. By being transparent and offering some reassurance and/or explanation of the use of caucus, mediators can reduce fears of bias that might otherwise grow.

Name the Problem

Mediators name the problem when one or more parties' behavior is being counterproductive to the goals of increasing mutual understanding and working toward a resolution. The logic behind this strategy is that awareness is a first step toward a change of attitude or behavior. Parties cannot stop behaviors or attitudes if they are not aware that they are hindering progress. Our mediators' advice is well summed up by mediator Bruce Engelbert: "[mediators need to] be direct and explain to the parties they do not seem to be making progress." Naming the problem can be tricky and mediators must do so with tact and appropriate timing.

How Mediators Name the Problem

The most straightforward way mediators can name the problem is to simply state to parties that something is not working. As mediator Maartje Van-der-Vlies says, "After hearing the stalemate ten times, it is pointed out to the combatants that nothing is happening." By drawing attention to the unproductive behaviors, mediators can generate ideas for alternative paths forward. Mediator Steven J. Gold says, "Once the dead horse has been beaten pretty thoroughly, I will focus on moving towards possible resolutions instead of continuing to go in circles." Another expert mediator shared his strategy: "I jokingly say, 'let's stop pretending this is going well.'"

Mediators may choose to illustrate the problem with a story or an analogy to change parties' attitude and appear less preachy. In fact, sometimes stories with a point are more effective than lectures. Stories also help to depersonalize the behavior and reduce the chance that either party will become defensive at being corrected or reprimanded by the mediator. Mediator John E. Sands elaborates this issue,

> I told this story of Nelson Mandela and Bill Clinton: showing Clinton the cell where he had spent 17 years, in response to Clinton's observation of how angry he must still be, Mandela replied, "When they told me I could go and I started to walk out, the anger welled up in me. Before I reached the door I realized that if I didn't let it go, I would be in prison my entire life. So I let it go."

When Naming the Problem is Appropriate

Naming the problem is mediators' preferred strategy when dealing with one party who is being difficult or when both parties are overwhelmed by the conflict. When naming the problem, it is important for mediators to explain their reasons for naming the behaviors and gain the parties' commitment to change those behaviors going forward. Mediator Rachel Fishman Green explains how she uses this strategy:

> [I will] discuss why mediation cannot continue if one person feels cut down—his/her voice will disappear—which has happened in a mediation case which I am now working on as a collaborative attorney. After the couple spent $4,000 with the mediator, the wife's voice had entirely disappeared from the room.

There is an important opportunity inherent in this strategy: by specifically discussing counterproductive behaviors, and by suggesting alternative behaviors, mediators can act as conflict coaches, empowering parties to learn new conflict resolution and communication skills that will serve them in the current dispute and in the future as well. This opportunity for skill development and empowerment is one of the spillover benefits that sometimes occur with mediation.

Risks of Naming the Problem

Naming the problem is a riskier strategy than the others discussed thus far. When using this strategy, mediators may wish to consider doing so in caucus to save face for the party whose behaviors are being singled out. If both parties' behaviors are problematic, then addressing them in joint session is less risky. While naming a counterproductive behavior can run the risk of appearing to erode the mediator's neutrality, it can also be an important turning point in mediation. By being transparent with the parties and letting them know that your goal is to facilitate productive negotiations, parties can often overcome their initial reticence to accept this as part of the mediator's neutrality.

Enforce Ground Rules

When one party tries to dominate, bully or mistreat the other party, mediators are forced to take on the role of moderator or referee, enforcing basic rules of civility in order to facilitate a productive discussion. The enforcement of ground rules can pose challenges for neutrality since their violation is nearly always a lopsided event, with one party in violation more frequently or flagrantly than the other(s). In such cases, mediators generally remind the parties that everyone will have a turn to speak and also reiterate how the process of mediation works. In many cases, this is sufficient to stop the unacceptable behaviors. When it is not, caucus may need to be used in order to work separately with a party who lacks self-control or has not fully committed to trying the mediation process.

How Mediators Enforce Ground Rules

The basic strategy for explaining ground rules is to list do's and dont's. For example, mediator Julie Barnes reports, "I remind them of their agreement at the beginning of mediation to treat each other with respect, listen, et cetera, and tell them that they will get their chance to say what they need to during their turn. If nothing else works, we may have to separate and caucus." In addition, it is important to get parties' commitment to these ground rules. Mediator Douglas E. Noll illustrates this point, "I obtain commitment to ground rules. When a behavior violates a ground rule I ask the party what his/her commitment is to the ground rule. That always stops the behavior. It is an application of creating social norms and expecting conformance to those new norms."

Sometimes, it is hard to keep parties' commitment to ground rules. In such cases, mediators should challenge transgressions. Mediator Douglas E. Noll illustrates this point: "[One] party insulted another party. I ask, 'That sounded inflammatory to me. What is your commitment to showing respect to everyone and this process?' It caused the party to reflect on his commitment and behavior which led to a rich conversation about the way the parties were treating each other." In extreme cases, it might be necessary for mediators to threaten to end mediation if unacceptable behaviors continue. Mediation should not become a venue for one party to abuse the other.

When Enforcing Ground Rules is Appropriate

The strategy of stressing ground rules is mostly used when mediators have to deal with one or both parties' inappropriate behavior. Here is the conundrum: if the mediator doesn't act, the victimized party may feel the mediator is biased. If the mediator protects one party, then the attacking party may perceive the mediator's action as biased. In these contentious cases, it can be helpful to list explicit ground rules (e.g., we will speak one at a time) and get at least a verbal commitment to follow those ground rules. Mediator Don Greenstein gives an example of how stressing ground rules can be used to control unacceptable behaviors:

> When one party raises their voice and yells abusively at the other party, I use a quiet and steady voice to ask the boisterous party to speak to me and explain what the outburst was about. I emphasize that mediation works best when people speak in a respectful manner. Is that something he or she can agree to? I'd then ask if they can proceed in joint session, and if another outburst occurs I'd go into separate sessions and ask the boisterous party more about their behavior and how it might serve or disserve them in reaching a resolution to the problem.

Risks of Enforcing Ground Rules

Stressing the ground rules is a low to moderately risky strategy in terms of the tendency to compromise neutrality in the eyes of one or more parties. Disputants generally accept that it is the mediator's job to act as a referee and enforce reasonable ground rules. This sounds perfectly reasonable in principal. Yet when one side is violating the ground rules more than the other side(s), which is usually the case, the transgressing party may misinterpret the mediator's behavior as a sign of bias. Therefore, when a party's behavior provokes the need for repeated corrections it may be best to separate the parties and address the situation in caucus. This allows the offending party to save face, rather than be reprimanded or reminded of the ground rules in joint session, thereby lowering the risk of perceived bias.

It should also be mentioned that these are instances in which mediators may actually develop a genuine dislike for or impatience with one side. It is difficult to remain opinion-free when faced with a party who refuses to listen or who mistreats others or the mediator. Most experienced mediators find ways to remain neutral and keep their opinions (if any) from showing. A common characteristic among experienced and successful mediators is an ability to maintain strong boundaries and refrain from becoming emotionally engaged when a party acts provocatively.

SUMMARY

As a general rule, mediators control the process while parties control the outcome. When one party takes control of the outcome because of a power imbalance, mediators should act. Conversely, when a party tries to take control of the process away from a mediator, he should also intervene. The challenge is to intervene without appearing biased. When expert mediators seek to address power imbalances, enforce ground rules, deal with difficult people, give reality checks, or deal with many of the other challenges arising in mediation, they run the risk of being viewed as biased for or against one side. Ironically, mediators must undertake these behaviors in order to be effective within the mediation session. Mediators must walk a fine line by accomplishing their role in a way that leaves the parties feeling respected, heard, and empowered. When this happens, claims of mediator bias are likely to be rare. Table 6.1 below summarizes how experienced mediators maintain neutrality while protecting the integrity of the mediation process and moving forward the search for joint solutions.

Table 6.1. Summary of Strategies to Maintain Neutrality

STRATEGIES	HOW?	WHEN?	RISK?
Explain Role in Strategies	*- Explain role* *- Confront perception*	*- When accused of being unfair* *- When one party challenges the mediator*	*- Mediator may feel vulnerable*
Reflect in Caucus	*- Isolate aggressor* *- Give time to think* *- Have high-power parties consider compromise*	*- One party is bullied by the other* *- One party needs time to process information*	*- May appear to be biased*
Name the Problem	*- State what is wrong* *- Use analogy*	*- Feeling of being right* *- Poor understanding of mediation*	*- Parties may lose face*
Enforce Ground Rules	*- Obtain commitment to ground rules* *- Challenge transgressions*	*- Dealing with a difficult party*	*- Transgressing parties may lose face*

Chapter Seven

Dealing with Parties' Emotions

Are you going to let her talk to my client that way?!

I don't care anymore. I will sign anything you put in front of me.

After what that company did to me and my family, they deserve to go bankrupt!

Mediation is nearly always an emotional process for the parties at the table, and sometimes for their representatives as well. Even novice mediators know that most parties come to mediation with high levels of emotionality surrounding their dispute. While family and divorce mediations regularly see emotionality arise as a challenge in mediation, it is also frequently an issue in commercial mediation, landlord tenant cases, and environmental dispute resolution. For these reasons, the mediators in our study listed emotionality as a significant challenge and cause of impasse in mediation.

Strong emotions create both opportunities and challenges during the mediation process. When parties are emotional, they are less likely to hold back on sharing their concerns at the mediation table. Their needs, concerns, and fears are close to the surface, allowing the mediator and the other parties to better understand the root of the problem from the perspective of the emotional party. Focusing on the dispute's emotional impact or unmet psychological and relational needs can lead to a breakthrough and a satisfying outcome. Mediator Andy G. Miller notes, "When parties are stuck, it is not usually because there is too much emotion, but because there is too little emotion."

On the other hand, strong emotions can interfere with a person's ability to listen to the other party, rationally process factual information, and engage in problem-solving behaviors (Druckman and Olekalns 2008). Badly managed emotions can lead to mediation impasse. Mediators must be comfortable with emotional displays, know how to harness emotions in the service of dispute resolution, understand how to defuse potentially volatile situations, know when to terminate mediation, and maintain strong personal boundaries that enable them to acknowledge the emotional concerns of others without becoming biased or overwhelmed by them.

WHY DOES DEALING WITH PARTIES' EMOTIONS POSE A CHALLENGE?

We asked mediators to be specific about the reasons why dealing with emotions can be a challenge to mediators and parties. Here is a story from mediator Robert J. McDonnell illustrating how emotion can affect the mediation process:

> With an older divorcing couple, the husband was physically ill and would need to leave the room to deal with his emotions. The wife would sit calmly while acknowledging that the situation was difficult. After a while, the husband would return to the session. He would participate but was obviously having a hard time with the divorce outcome.

As this example suggests, emotion can play a role by making parties uncomfortable in dealing with each other or with the problem. In some extreme cases, emotions can make parties unable to participate in the mediation process. Our panel of mediators gave us four main reasons why dealing with parties' emotions can be challenging in mediation: discomfort with emotions, the issue mattering more to one party than the other, different emotional styles, and the fear of being wronged (see Figure 7.1).

Discomfort with Emotion

The most common challenge when dealing with parties' emotions, as highlighted by our mediators, is the level of discomfort that some parties feel. Our mediators observed that the challenges stemming from differing comfort levels can result in a number of emotional reactions and may lead to a sudden impasse or withdrawal from the mediation process.

Some individuals are simply not comfortable expressing their emotions or being present while others do so. As mediator Vivian Berger points out, "People express anger and other negative emotions very differently, and some people have access to feelings more easily. Also, some people feel that

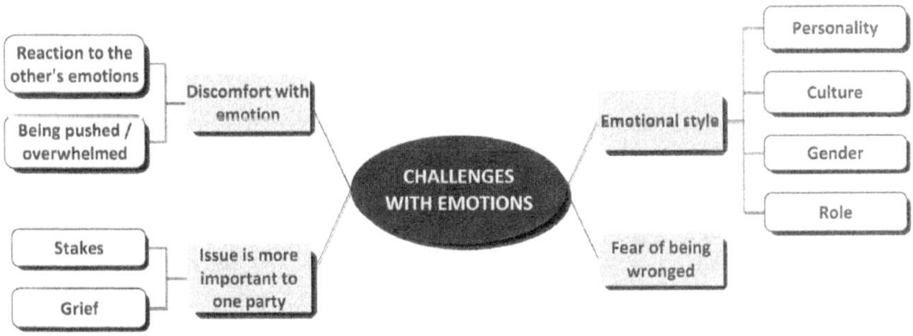

Figure 7.1. Mind map of reasons why emotions may pose a challenge

to show feelings is to show weakness." Comfort with emotions can also be related to levels of emotional intelligence, self-awareness, and maturity. As mediator Douglass E. Noll sums up, "Different tolerances for anxiety and different experiences of the conflict impact differences in emotional reactions."

Parties may also be uncomfortable with conflict if they are not certain what their reaction will be to the other party's emotions. According to mediator David Lichter, "People often do not like direct confrontation; they might not be prepared for what they are going to hear." Some parties fear their own reaction to the other party's emotional display. For example, a party may fear that they or the other party will lose their temper or break down emotionally. In these cases, a party might end mediation rather than take the chance that their own emotions will get out of control or further escalate the situation.

Finally, parties who are uncomfortable with emotional displays may feel fearful, trapped, even forced to listen to the other's venting. Parties may feel that the other's strong emotional expression might push them to a concession they would not otherwise make; this can make them less willing to be present during these emotional displays. In other words, parties may be afraid that emotion will be used as a negotiation strategy. As mediator Don Greenstein states, "[Often] parties feel pushed by the other person and are hurt or angry."

Issue is More Important to One Party

Sometimes parties become emotional due to the disputed issue's impact on their lives. As mediator Rachel Fishman Green points out, "People are making important decisions that will affect their whole futures, so it is very normal to have strong emotions." As a rule of thumb, the greater the dispute's potential to threaten one's livelihood and needs, the greater the fight or flight response will be. As mediator David Lichter explains, "The matters at hand can involve one's life's work in a business or the severing or damaging of very close personal or working relationships, which people can take very personally." The importance of the stakes will be directly related to the emotional charge the parties attach to issues.

While the stakes can be obvious, as with money needed to survive, in some cases, stakes can be related to psychological needs. In this regard, Maslow's hierarchy of needs (1943) suggests that the need for friendship, love, and self-esteem can be more important to people than basic needs. As one expert mediator reports, "In the workplace, a common unmet need causing conflict is respect. Naming the underlying need, like respect, brings obvious recognition and relief to participants, and they are usually ready to move on after the need is explicitly identified and they confirm it."

Another reason for strong emotions related to issues in mediation is grief. Sometimes parties in mediation do not have enough time to grieve the loss of important things. In such cases, they may not be ready to move on. The problem can be compounded when one party is further along in the grief process and thus more eager to move on than the other party. In a divorce, for example, usually one party has already started the process of recreating or visualizing his or her identity as a single person. The fact that the spouses are in two different places on this journey can be a source of conflict, as it is difficult for each of them to understand the other's worldview or outlook. Mediator Rachel Fishman Green comments on this phenomenon: "It is typical, in divorce, that one person is the initiator and the other is catching up, emotionally. The initiator has usually been unhappy in the marriage for a long time, and has been preparing to separate, while to the other it comes as a shock that the spouse wanted to separate."

Emotional Styles

When parties do not deal with emotions similarly, there is room for misunderstanding and dysfunctional communication, as parties may focus more on style than substance. Emotional style may vary between parties for many reasons. Firstly, personality can play a big role in parties' emotional styles. Mediator Rachel Fishman Green points out, "The more linear-thinking person is very impatient with the needs of the other person to express emotion, and does not want to pay for the time wasted in mediation expressing emotion."

Secondly, individual emotional styles and conflict management modes are influenced by one's family or cultures (Neuliep 2009). For example, each family has unwritten rules through which it communicates the appropriate ways to deal with problems or conflicts (Wilmot and Hocker 2000). For some families, the appropriate way to react to conflict is to avoid it at all costs in an effort to maintain harmonious relationships. People coming from this type of conflict orientation are likely to be highly uncomfortable talking openly about problems, especially in the presence of a stranger (i.e., the mediator), yet passive-aggressive behavior such as pouting or the silent treatment is acceptable. On the other end of the spectrum are families that see conflict as an opportunity for competition, with the goal being to win the argument at all costs. In competitive families, it is acceptable to tell someone exactly what you are thinking without concern for the other's feelings or ego. The rules in competitive conflict cultures say that if someone has a problem with you, they will tell you about it directly. Those who do not engage in these battles are weak.

Thirdly, gender can also play a role in emotional style. Researchers have long been able to track general differences in expressiveness and communication styles between men and women that impact the expression of emotion during mediation (Neuliep 2009; Tannen 1990; Brown and Gilligan 1992). When feeling powerless, males tend to state their position and offer logical reasons to support it (Watson 1994). In contrast, women tend to choose responses based on interpersonal obligations (Wilmot and Hocker 2001). In workplace settings, research has shown men to be more conflict avoidant than women (Folger, Poole, and Stutman 2001). Mediator Susan Zaidel explains gender difference in mediation:

> In divorce mediation, there is a gender difference, with women more expressive of emotions and men preferring to focus on problem-solving the issues. For women, feelings are an important part of the process of discussing the issues, but for men it often seems like a side issue or even irrelevant to the objective topic being discussed.

Lastly, expert mediators found that individuals in mediation also exhibited differences in their emotional expressions due to their role identities. One's role identity as a parent, employee, business owner, or insurance company representative has a large impact on emotional expression in mediation. Managers come to mediation to represent their companies. Any financial settlement will come out of their company's pockets, and the dispute is therefore less threatening to their economic or psychic well-being than to the employee who feels he or she has been treated unfairly or injured on the job. For employees, the impact of the dispute is usually much more personal. As mediator John E. Sands points out, "Many people invest a great deal of their self-esteem in their work, and the impact on their families is significant." As a rule of thumb, the closer the client is to the dispute itself, the greater the likelihood that it will evoke strong emotions. Mediator Robert Leitch summarizes this principle:

> This [emotionality] usually depends on whether the parties are regular people or professionals. What I mean is that people who often participate in negotia-

tions or mediations, such as business people, insurance adjusters, or other frequent mediation attendees, are usually less affected by the emotional outbursts of the other side.

Fear of Being Wronged

Expert mediators in our study stated that parties are often fearful of being wronged again by a party who has betrayed them, let them down, or left them out of the loop in the past. As mediator Georgia Geiger illustrates, "[Often] parties may feel that they are not being heard or that they are not being respected." Sometimes the hurt may be related to deeper wounds. Mediator Don Greenstein reports, "[Parties'] strong emotions, at least strong negative ones, tend to be driven by an underlying sense of being wronged (victimized), hurt, or placed in a fearful situation." The field of behavioral psychology teaches us that humans learn patterns of responses to conflict based on past experiences. If a party believes the other side has let them down or mistreated them in the past, they will not only show fear, pain, regret, and mistrust, they will also avoid a repeat of the previous problems, either by avoiding that person altogether or by seeking to punish that person for past wrongs.

Preferred Strategies to Deal with Parties' Emotions

Although it is quite challenging, expert mediators are unanimous: emotion cannot be ignored. According to our panel of expert mediators, strategies to deal with emotions can range from giving space for emotional expression to helping parties deal with emotion, or focusing on a goal to help parties move beyond the emotional roadblock. Along the way, expert mediators also coach parties on dealing with emotions, identify underlying needs, and help parties better understand the other's emotional struggle.

Give Space for Emotional Expression

The basic strategy that expert mediators use to deal with parties' emotions is giving space for emotional expression. Even if the emotions seem to be moving the discussion further away from the negotiation of specific agreements, mediators noted that the emotions should be legitimized and then used to help resolve conflict. Mediator Doug Thompson summed this principle up, saying, "I allow people to own the emotion and why it exists, and hopefully share what they want in an effort to move forward." Expert mediators also agreed that emotion must be expressed in order to help parties move forward. Mediator Rachel Fishman Green concurs, "I accept all emotions. They have to come out and be fully expressed before we will be able to have a settlement."

How Mediators Give Space for Emotional Expression

Expert mediators use various strategies to help parties deal with emotions. The first strategy that the mediator can use to give space to emotional expression is simply encouraging parties to express their emotions. Many of our mediators' suggestions dealt with the need to make space for emotions by normalizing the presence and expression of strong emotions in mediation. By normalizing the presence of emotions in the conflict resolution process, mediators can put emotional clients at ease and encourage them to express their concerns in an authentic way. One expert mediator summarizes his strategy as, "[I try] to show sympathy for the person expressing emotion, saying that having and expressing feelings is normal and OK."

A second strategy is setting up formal or informal ground rules that help make space for emotional expression. Ground rules often help define the line between constructive emotional expressions, which clarify needs and share one's perspective, and destructive emotional expressions, which include name-calling, blame casting, and other escalatory behaviors. Mediator Vivian Berger puts it simply: "I stress that we are here to listen to each others' honest feelings, so long as expression is not unduly abusive. I indicate such expression is where we begin, hopefully not where we end up. It is a step on the road to resolution." Ground rules will not only help parties feel comfortable expressing their emotions, they will also make parties feel comfortable listening to emotion. According to mediator Tony Newport, "Emotional expression is invariably valuable to the mediator and, if it is handled well, can give the non-emotive party a sense of confidence that the mediation will not be hijacked by the other party's feelings."

Some parties take longer to compose themselves, to explain how we got here, to formulate their proposals to one another, and to weigh and respond to proposals. As a result, a third strategy when giving space to emotional expression is explaining to the less emotional party the reasons why the mediator is allowing time for venting, explanations of past events, et cetera. Mediators explain that the purpose of this slower pace is to give parties the chance to explain how they feel and what they need (e.g., express their interests). Mediator Susan Zaidel summarizes this principle: "The pace needs to accommodate the party who is less ready for the divorce (the more emotional one) but, while the feelings must be acknowledged, the focus will be on the issues that need to be resolved."

Similarly, a fourth strategy is to help parties understand the value of expressing emotions in mediation. Mediators may need to explain that mediation agreements can involve both monetary and nonmonetary provisions; they may also have to clarify the link between a party's emotional expression and settlement in mediation. This helps the less emotional party understand the direct link between emotional needs and settlement agreements. As one expert mediator puts it, "[It is important] to explain that unexpressed emotions are likely to impede progress in negotiation and that letting others get things off their chest is helpful in getting past a possible impediment to settlement."

Giving or making space for emotional expression is a strategy that combines well with the use of caucus. This can be especially useful when one party needs to vent but the other is not ready to hear it. In such cases, allowing a party to express his emotions in private to the mediator can still be useful to help move things forward without alienating the other party. As mediator Sally Lord states, "[It] depends on the emotion and whether it can actually be channeled to focus them. Sometimes an opportunity for a private session with the mediator to *vent* can be helpful."

When Giving Space to Emotional Expression is Appropriate

Expert mediators use the strategy of giving space to emotional expression when one party feels he or she has been wronged. As mentioned earlier, strong emotions often come to the surface when a participant in mediation feels mistreated or wronged by the other party. Expressing this frustration is often a necessary step in moving the process forward. Mediator Douglas E. Noll offers an example of how this strategy can be used:

> Two women were in litigation over the sale of a business. As I heard the story of the plaintiff, she was obviously angry. As I asked her about the anger, she said that winning was everything to her, and she could not stand to see her former business partner succeed in the business without her. We worked through all of the emotions, getting finally to a place where the plaintiff had felt abandoned and unloved. Once that was unpacked, the case quickly resolved.

As mentioned earlier, the use of caucus can be helpful to create space for expressing emotions. When high emotions lead to high levels of destructive conflict, the mediators in our study most frequently used a caucus to avoid escalation and impasse. When emotions turn the tone of a session from constructive to destructive, most mediators turn to the use of caucus session. Mediator Jerry Wood relates how caucus was used to help parties express emotions:

> This case involved a male party and a female party, both *pro se* representations. During her opening, the woman broke down and wept openly. The male rolled his eyes and looked very peeved. He then stared off into space and tuned out. I offered a tissue to both parties and walked over to the ice chest and got us all a bottle of water. Then I sat down without comment and waited for the opening to continue. She continued with her opening, and he listened. After reframing the issues and setting the agenda, I then caucused with both sides to

see whether they were willing and able to engage in joint problem solving. The female showed no reservations, but the male was uncomfortable with going back into joint session. I told each of them that either could call for a caucus at any time. Both wanted to resolve the issue, and both felt that they could make more progress in a joint session. Both agreed to engage in joint problem solving.

Risks of Giving Space for Emotional Expression

In nearly all cases, giving the parties the space they need to express their emotions and concerns is a low-risk strategy. In their introductory remarks, mediators usually explain that each side will be able to speak without interruption, share their concerns, and make proposals. There are times when this strategy may veer into the moderately risky zone. For example, if the less emotional party or his attorney feels attacked by the other party's destructive venting of emotions, they may decide to terminate the mediation. Additionally, less emotional parties may become impatient with the slower pace of mediation necessitated by the emotional party's needs. They may also become uncomfortable with the mediator showing empathy toward the other party. When that occurs, the mediator must work with the less emotional party and explain why it is important and helpful to allow the expression of emotion. Caucus can also be used by the mediator to avoid looking biased while allowing a party to express his emotions.

Help Parties Understand Emotions

Mediators also play a crucial role by helping parties understand each other's emotional needs. There are a number of ways in which mediators help parties understand both the need for emotional expression and the content of emotional expressions. Whether in caucus or joint session, the basic principle is to encourage listening, understanding, and sympathy between the parties, while reframing statements as necessary and showing how to respect the feelings of others during the mediation process.

How Mediators Help Parties Understand Emotions

To help parties better understand each other's emotional state and needs, expert mediators adopt the role of translator. Mediator Doug Thompson summarizes this strategy: "[I] help the parties see and understand sentiments being expressed by others. The party less visibly expressing emotion may in fact feel just as deeply about it but is simply not as much on the sleeve. Mediators act by reframing, summarizing, and affirming these expressions among other things." When trust between parties is low, they will often undervalue offers coming from the other side through a process known as reactive devaluation. The mediator may therefore need to translate one side's offer or needs for the other side in order for it to be truly heard.

Mediators should occasionally reframe expressions of emotion in order to make the emotions less threatening. Translating parties' emotional needs can also be done in caucus, if expressions must be drastically reframed, or if parties need to save face. An expert mediator summarizes his strategy as follows: "[I try to] neutralize the language and reframe in order to convey the message. If the emotional expression is making the session unproductive, private sessions may become necessary as a last resort."

When Helping to Understand Emotions is Appropriate

Expert mediators like to help parties understand emotions when one or both parties are uncomfortable with emotional expression. Helping understand emotions is particularly useful when one party is highly vocal but unclear about his emotions, while the other party is shut down by the emotional display. One expert mediator told us about a wonderful mediation case that illustrates how helping parties understand can break impasses:

> In a small court case a few years ago, an African-American woman in her late 60s to early 70s became very emotional while relating the circumstances leading to the dispute with the vendor for a commercial coffeemaker she purchased on behalf of her church group. The storeowner was dismissive, accused her of breaking the machine through ignorance, and refused to cooperate with her when she sought to exchange the machine she purchased for a new one. During her recitation of her experience, she expressed emotional dimensions to her experience of the storeowner, although she never explicitly articulated a basis for her emotional charge. The store owner, a white man with a German accent, became frustrated with the woman's emotional storytelling, and challenged the emotional dimensions of the issues and insisted upon addressing the strict commercial elements of the dispute. When summarizing to the parties, I started with a brief review of the plaintiff's story, a brief review of the defendant's demand to stick to facts not emotions, and then asked the plaintiff to explain her emotional reaction. She then started to talk about her multiple efforts to speak to the defendant, his sales staff's insistence on having the receipt in hand although the store's sticker was on the box, which necessitated several trips to the store and back, and his use of the words *you people* when describing how the defendant storeowner replied to her explanations of what happened when the commercial coffeemaker broke. I reflected back what I thought was being left unsaid: that she experienced this as a form of racism. She readily agreed, then detailed her long involvement in the Civil Rights struggle as an educated woman fighting oppression and deprivation. The storeowner was taken aback by this, having failed to appreciate the basis for the plaintiff's emotional reaction. He then explained *you people* referred to *all* people who buy commercial products but then don't know how to use them properly. He apologized profusely for the misunderstanding, and the plaintiff and defendant then worked out a mutually satisfactory resolution that gave the

plaintiff the coffeemaker she needed and the defendant the opportunity to repair a relationship with a potentially good institutional client (the church for which the plaintiff purchased the coffeemaker in the first place).

Risks of Helping Parties Understand Emotions

There is very little risk in explaining why emotional expression is important to the mediation process or why one party may express himself differently than the other in mediation. Mediators may need to choose their words carefully when they describe the other side's style and use caucus so as to avoid offending the more emotional party. For example, if one party is angry and blaming the other side for the problems that gave rise to the mediation, then the mediator may wish to use caucus for two purposes: first, to allow the angry party to vent without causing unnecessary conflict escalation, and second, to explain to the less angry party that the other side needs to get some things off his chest before the mediation can move forward with problem solving. Mediators must also choose their words to avoid seeming biased toward a weepy, vulnerable party or against an angry, hostile party.

Identify Underlying Needs and Interests

Sometimes, the parties talk openly about their need for an apology, a change in future behavior from the other party or other nonfinancial compensation, or even revenge. More often, emotional needs are not expressed directly. There are many reasons parties may not state their needs openly: they are afraid of looking weak, they might wrongly assume the other is aware of their needs, or they may be grappling with emotions and unable to express themselves clearly. By uncovering the parties' needs, it becomes possible to work together on possible solutions.

How Mediators Identify Underlying Needs and Interests

The basic strategy expert mediators use to identify needs is to help parties convert their emotions into openly stated needs. The procedure is straightforward: help parties recognize their emotions and then probe for frustrated needs. An expert mediator describes his approach as follows: "For me, the expression of emotion is one way that someone expresses his or her underlying needs. I am always looking to identify parties' needs, so I validate the emotional expression, explicitly identify the need, and get confirmation from the participant."

Sometimes, identifying needs is easier in private caucus with parties. This is especially true when one party is afraid to look weak or is struggling with the meaning of his emotions. In such cases, a private meeting will provide the face-saving essentials for a meaningful conversation. One expert mediator agreed, saying, "If one person is less emotionally expressive, identifying needs will require more of my skills, and listening even more to what is being said or unsaid. If not already planning a caucus, I will use a caucus to identify the needs of each participant."

When Identifying Underlying Needs and Interests is Appropriate

Identifying underlying needs is appropriate in every case and is foundational to Fisher and Ury's (1981) key concept of interests. Interests are the needs that underlie positions. The most satisfying solutions occur when interests are met. An emotional disputant is likely to have interests that go beyond mere financial settlements. He may want an apology, a promise of changed behavior in the future, or some other form of nonmonetary compensation. He may feel that his basic security and identity have been threatened by the actions of the other party, or by the litigation process itself. It is important to uncover the need, fear, or concern that lies beneath an emotional outburst. An expert mediator relates a story that illustrates this strategy:

> The husband was angry because his wife habitually overspends. The mediator addresses the cause of the overspending and finds out that she does it to try to get the husband's attention because he doesn't pay any attention to her. Now the mediator can help the parties work on lots of methods to address the basic problem and simultaneously take away the anger.

Sometimes, both parties are aware of the needs, but one party does not fully understand how important the issue is to the other. This is especially true when a party feels betrayed or let down. In such cases, mediators should help the party fully assess the importance of the other's need. Mediator Doug Thompson illustrates this strategy:

> One party was angry because he felt his professional reputation had been impugned by the other party. That other party felt that it was an issue in the past, 'let's just forget it, and move on.' The mediator's role was to help the let's move on party see that moving ahead could be most efficiently accomplished by clearing the air and helping him see that the alleged insults were not easily put aside by the first party because they struck at some important questions of identity.

Risks of Identifying Underlying Needs and Interests

Asking open-ended questions is generally a low-risk strategy to get at the underlying needs and interests of emotional parties. When parties are highly emotional, mediators must be particularly careful in choosing their words. A poorly chosen word or an unartful framing may make the emotional party believe the mediator is biased or unsympathetic. For example, "I can tell this is upsetting. Can you share more information with me about why you feel this way or how we might improve the situation in the future?" sounds very different than, "What's there to cry about?" Upset parties are already more likely to terminate mediation, so the mediator needs to choose words carefully in striving to learn more about the underlying interests of each party. The biggest risk to mediation occurs when the underlying needs and interests are not discovered by the mediator and understood by all parties. When parties get stuck in positional bargaining (e.g., I won't take a penny less than $50,000), we do not learn enough about their true needs to fully address the conflict. Ask open-ended questions and find the answers to such questions as "How did you arrive at that number?" or, "What need does that amount meet for you?" or better yet, "If you got that entire amount today, would you feel like the harm had been fully repaired?"

Coaching Parties to Deal with Emotions

Whether it occurs in caucus or joint session, many mediators take on the role of coach when they find that a particular skill or piece of conflict resolution knowledge may be helpful in furthering constructive dialogue. The objective is to make sure that, at least, parties do not hinder the process by responding inappropriately, and at best they help by responding appropriately.

How Mediators Coach Parties to Deal with Emotions

The mediators in our study shared a variety of methods for coaching parties to deal constructively with emotions. Firstly, they discuss techniques for self-regulation, anger management, and overall mastery of emotional expression. The overarching goal is to help parties to not become overwhelmed by emotions. In this regard, venting in caucus with the mediator can be necessary. Mediator David Lichter illustrates this point,

> I let the party vent, exhibit understanding and sympathy with the party's position, and then explain to them that they have to try to put the emotion aside to make what amounts to a rational business decision to get the matter resolved. Sometimes I also try to explain that the system cannot deliver at the end of the process what some very emotional people sometimes think they want: an apology, a public scolding, or some sort of vindication other than dollars.

They may also coach parties to better express their emotions in mediation. Expressions of anger or frustration are generally tolerated, but not when they deteriorate and become destructive. In caucus, expert mediators coach parties to express their emotions in a constructive manner. Mediator John E. Sands explains his strategy, "I address it with the reluctant participant in caucus and then practice dealing with the emotional issue with a role-playing exercise in mediation."

Lastly, they may work with parties on empathy skills by modeling and describing helpful behaviors. During this coaching, the mediator often reminds the parties about basic ground rules that generally preclude name-calling and personal attacks. Sometimes, the goal is simply to coach the party to not overreact to the other's expression of emotions. As mediator Robert Leitch explains, "I try to get each to recognize that the other is just who he or she is and, with or without the mediation, that will not change. And you each need to deal with it, just as you would with anyone you deal with elsewhere—at work, in your family, etc."

When Coaching to Deal with Emotions is Appropriate

Expert mediators use coaching when parties' emotional styles can hinder the process. Usually coaching is helpful with parties that tend to express feelings too strongly. The objective of such coaching is to help the party better restrain himself or express his needs more appropriately. An expert mediator gives an example of coaching:

> The first party brought a civil action in damages against the other for cutting some trees that he claimed were part of his property. He was angry, and at the end of his opening, he called the other party a thief. Before the other could respond, I asked the speaker if he remembered the promise he made to abide by the ground rules about not making personal comments about the other party during mediation. He said 'yes' and he apologized to me and the other party. The other party remained calm, accepted the apology and stated that according to a surveyor that he had hired before he began cutting, the trees appeared to be on his property. A compromise was reached.

Sometimes the coaching will be about making a more introverted party comfortable dealing with an extroverted party. The objective of such coaching is to help the party better deal with the other's emotions or better react to what is said. The idea is to help parties cope with the other's emotional charges. An expert mediator offers an example of this strategy:

> Two clients in a workplace dispute were discussing options for resolving the issues. The employee, who was from a very emotionally expressive culture and also had a background in theater arts, was using her hands as she spoke. Her voice became louder as she became more excited and she began to move around the conference room rather than staying seated. The supervisor stopped talking, physically shrunk down in his chair, and appeared to be intimidated. I named what I was observing, captured the options that were being generated, and ended up meeting privately with the parties to discover that the supervisor had no experience with physically expressive cultures and was actually afraid

of his employee due to an unrelated event from his childhood that reminded him of the employee.

Risks of Coaching to Deal with Emotions

Coaching parties to improve their ability to deal with emotions varies from low to moderately risky, depending on the personality and emotional state of the parties and the framings employed by the mediator. If they are not careful, mediators may come off as *preachy* or patronizing in their attempts to coach parties on their communication or coping skills. Mediators may wish to preface their remarks with an explanation as to why the coaching is likely to help (perhaps without even calling it coaching). Coaching is often done in caucus, unless the skill development needs are shared equally by the parties, in which case it may be done more effectively in joint session.

Focus on a Goal

After the parties have had a chance to vent and share concerns in caucus or joint session, they sometimes get stuck and cannot seem to move toward the next phase of the process. Beer and Stief (1997) call this the *gerbil wheel*: parties go around and around but they do not get anywhere. It feels good to tell their story to someone who will listen (usually the mediator). They get mired in storytelling and retelling. As a mediator, when you have heard the same complaint voiced two or more times, this is an indication the party may be stuck on the gerbil wheel. When emotional venting and expression seems to have become endless and repetitive, it is time to refocus the parties on the goal of mediation, which is problem solving.

How Mediators Focus Parties on the Goal

Expert mediators use various strategies to shift parties' attention toward finding a solution. A first strategy to help parties focus on a goal is to nudge them towards a more forward-focused discussion of potential solutions. It usually consists of reframing the conversation toward the outcome of mediation. Reframing can be general, as mediator Georgia Geiger shows, "[I] remind parties that mediation is future-oriented. 'What would you prefer the situation to look like from now on?'" Reframing can also be very specific, as mediator Sally Lord illustrates when she says, "[I] focus the parties on the children's needs."

When reframing is not enough, expert mediators indicated they use a specific technique called backcasting. This technique asks parties to imagine an ideal future in which the dispute has been resolved to everyone's satisfaction; relationships have been restored, when applicable. Then it asks them to consider the steps it would take to get to that ideal future. When parties are stuck complaining about how they feel, backcasting can be a powerful way to help parties move to the next phase of the mediation process. An expert mediator explains this strategy when, "I say to the parties: 'Skip to the future. Ask what a good resolution would look like down the road. Picture yourself looking back on today. What advice would you give yourself if you could?'"

When Focusing on the Goal is Appropriate

When a party's emotional style prevents him or her from moving beyond complaints, expert mediators usually help this party move forward by refocusing mediation on a goal. Such strategies should be used when parties have had a chance to express their needs and feelings to the mediator and the other party. One expert mediator illustrated how focusing on a goal can help a party move forward:

> A father was so mad at his ex that he was unable to address the substance of a contempt action. He just wanted to rehash the whole failed marriage and the way he was wronged. In caucus, I asked him to tell me about his son: how old, what did they like to do together, what did he want his son to grow up to be? Then I asked him to picture himself in his grown-up son's house looking back on this mediation; what would you tell yourself? He grinned and said: "I guess I would tell myself to man up and do the right thing."

Risks of Focusing Parties on the Goal

Focusing parties on a goal to help them move beyond emotional entanglement can be a risky strategy if done poorly. First, parties may feel that the mediator is not empathetic at all and lose trust in him or her. If a party has not had a chance to fully share his feelings and concerns, he may feel that the mediator is rushing him. Secondly, for some parties, the emotional concern is the primary issue at stake in the mediation. If so, the mediator's future focus needs to be centered on relational rather than simply monetary terms, so the party feels she is not being slighted. If the mediator seems to have a myopic focus on settlement to the exclusion of the parties' emotional needs and concerns, they might become alienated from the process and terminate the mediation.

SUMMARY

Our mediators found that emotionality occurs relatively frequently, and highly emotional cases tend to take longer to mediate. High levels of emotion can lead to conflict escalation or termination of the process by one or more parties or by the mediator, if unaddressed. Although discomfort with emotions is the first thing that comes to mind when we talk about the challenge of emotions, our panel of mediators reported several other situations that can be problematic. More specifically, parties' emotional styles, the asymmetric importance of issues, and the feeling of being wronged can all be difficult. Expert mediators suggested a number of strategies to address the challenges posed by emotionality in the mediation process, including giving space for emotional expression, helping parties understand each other's emotions, identifying underlying needs, coaching, and helping parties to focus on a goal. Table 7.1 below summarizes strategies used by mediators to deal with parties' emotions.

Table 7.1. Summary of Strategies to Deal with Parties' Emotion

STRATEGIES	HOW?	WHEN?	RISK?
Give Space to Emotional Expression	*- Encourage emotional expression* *- Set up ground rules* *- Give time to express oneself* *- Explain the role of emotions* *- Use caucus*	*- Feeling of being wronged*	*- Being perceived as patronizing* *- Being perceived as taking sides*
Help Parties Understand the Other's Emotions	*- «Translate» emotion*	*- Discomfort with emotions*	*- Being perceived as patronizing* *- Being perceived as taking sides*
Identify Underlying Needs	*- Probe emotions* *- Use caucus*	*- Issues are more important to one party*	*- Being perceived as patronizing*
Coach Parties to Deal with Emotions	*- Self-regulation* *- Rehearsal* *- Empathy modeling*	*- Differing emotional style*	*- Being perceived as patronizing* *- Being perceived as taking sides*
Focus on a Goal	*- Reframe toward resolution* *- Backcasting*	*- Differing emotional style* *- Level of comfort with emotions*	*- Being perceived as being non-empathetic* *- Being perceived as taking sides*

Chapter Eight

Moving from Past to Future Focus

How can I negotiate with someone who has treated me so badly?

We have never worked well together. I can't imagine that is going to change.

Until he admits this is his fault, I can't negotiate with him.

When mediation ends in an impasse, it is frequently due to the parties' inability to move from a past to a future focus. While these obstacles are often rooted in emotional needs rather than objective valuations of the case, it should be noted there are indeed times when one party has been victimized by the other (e.g., domestic violence, theft, vandalism, et cetera). In these cases, it may be important for the offender to acknowledge past transgressions and to apologize before a future-oriented discussion is appropriate. However, even in cases where criminal offenses have not occurred, parties sometimes keep focusing on having been wronged by the other.

When a party is stuck in the past, he will not tell his story just once (and it will be a story in which he was the victim of the other party or parties). Instead, he may repeat himself in various ways, rehashing the story from his perspective over and over again. In other cases, the party will be overtly passive or disorganized in mediation, as they cannot engage in the process of moving forward.

The problem with being stuck in the past is that mediation is not about the past, but about the future. The moment when parties take the leap from sharing their stories of what happened in the past to discussing what they hope will change in the future is a critical juncture in the mediation process

(Haynes, Haynes, and Fong 2004). The mediation process is at its best at the moment when the conflict begins to transform from a story about frustration, anger, or betrayal to one of possibilities, hope, and change. This does not mean past events or transgressions are unimportant, but that the parties must be able to transition to a future-oriented discussion for mediation to result in settlement.

Mediators are frequently frustrated by parties who are stuck in the past and unable to consider options for a better future. It is also a significant factor in mediation impasses. Luckily, experienced mediators have found ways of helping parties move from being stuck in the past to looking forward in mediation. This chapter will examine the reasons why parties might be stuck and propose strategies to help parties engage in problem solving.

HOW PARTIES BECOME STUCK IN THE PAST

We asked mediators to elaborate on the reasons why parties may become stuck in the past, as well as how being stuck can impair the mediation process. While it is a challenging skill to develop, helping parties move from past to future is necessary to break impasse most of the time. A wonderful story from mediator Susan V. Edwards illustrates how helping parties become unstuck can break impasse:

> A case that should have been simple went on for two-and-a-half years. The husband was very organized and always well prepared. The wife's documents were an increasingly large mare's nest of paper. She was never prepared. As they were not moving forward (the wife's disorganization was her passive-aggressive resistance to the divorce), I met with the parties, their lawyers, and psychologists in a five-way meeting. With their attorneys and psychologists encouraging them, the wife eventually accepted reality (including that the husband was giving her considerably more than a court would have given her and the cost of going to court was prohibitive). The wife finally accepted the husband's spreadsheets and proposal (with a few adjustments to address some of her own personal needs). She needed the entire two-and-a-half years to be ready to move on.

According to our panel of expert mediators, parties become stuck for different reasons. Mostly, parties become stuck because they want to hold the other responsible or because they are not ready to deal with issues. In some cases, parties focus on the past because they want their pain to be recognized, or worse, because the conflict has become their life (see Figure 8.1).

The Other Party Must be Responsible

According to our expert mediators, a major reason why it is difficult to move from a past to a future focus is because one or more parties blame the other for the problem. As one expert mediator explains, "The parties want vindication for their emotions and to know they are right." Moreover, being the victim may create a comfortable narrative. Unfortunately, blaming others may help bolster one's identity as a victim and the victim status makes it hard to acknowledge any level of personal responsibility.

Another reason is that parties may fear a loss of face by admitting to the mediator, to the other party, or even to themselves that they had some agency in the dispute or its longevity. Parties may also be afraid that admitting some level of responsibility for the dispute may weaken their legal case. Mediator Daniel E. Gulden makes this point: "Not blaming the other party may make the blamer feel at fault. That feeling may be hard to accept. The blamer may, on his or her own or upon an attorney's advice, feel their bargaining position could be weakened by accepting some responsibility."

Finally, sometimes a party hopes to claim victim status in order to gain favor with the mediator. By painting themselves as the victims, they do not have to take any responsibility for the dispute and they might seem more sympathetic to outsiders. Mediator Susan V. Edwards summarizes this point, "They hope they'll find a sympathetic ear from the mediator. I also think they believe they can sway the mediator to guide the decision-making process to favor them."

Parties Want their Pain to be Recognized

When parties come into mediation, they generally do not feel their experiences have been acknowledged. Parties may need to vent their anger, sad-

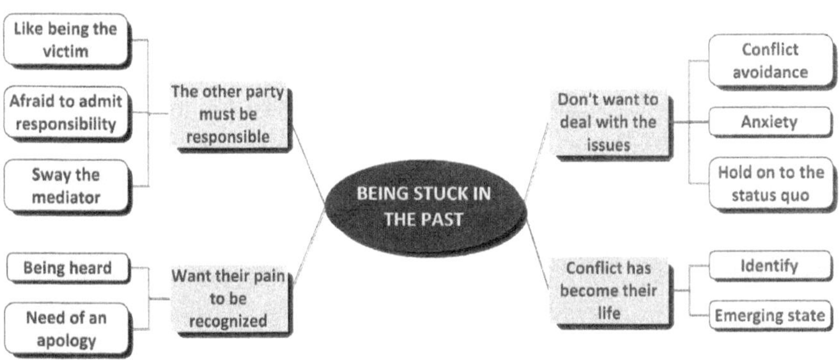

Figure 8.1. Mind map of reasons why parties may be stuck in the past

ness, or fear in order to move on. In such cases, parties often express a need for the mediator and/or the other party to acknowledge their pain and to hear them. A first degree of recognition would be for these parties to have the other be aware of their pain. As mediator Ericka Gray points out, "They need to talk about the past, to have someone hear the stories." A second degree would be for these parties to demand an apology or need the other party to acknowledge the veracity of their perspective or narrative.

When one party refuses to acknowledge the pain, the hurt party may stress how wrong the other side is, either to the mediator or to the judge. They do this by telling their story in a way that focuses on what the dispute has meant for them, how it has impacted their lives, and how they had no culpability. Mediator Madeleine Sauvé explained this phenomenon: "Experiences of being misunderstood, dismissed, and unvalued create a general sense of unfairness for the parties. In the absence of any acknowledgement of their reality, they are compelled to highlight how the other is responsible for the current state. If the other's negative evaluation is wrong then perhaps their experiences will be heard with respect."

The Parties Do Not Want to Deal with the Issues

Parties may have difficulty negotiating a solution because they simply do not want to address the problem. This can occur because an individual has a conflict avoidant personality or because remaining in a state of psychological denial is emotionally safer than taking the risk of moving from the familiar role of victim to the unfamiliar role of collaborator. As mediator Douglas E. Noll points out, "Focusing on the past is comfortable, while looking at the future may produce anxiety and fear."

Another reason is that some disputants simply cannot envision a path forward that would result in a better future or a resolution to what has become an all-encompassing conflict. In parties' minds, the conflict is too big to be negotiated. As mediator Madeleine Sauvé observes, "[Parties] are not optimistic. They have not imagined there is a possibility of success." Focusing on the past or present may feel more comfortable than breaking this pattern to pursue a radically different future. In other words, parties have become comfortable with being in conflict. An expert mediator summarizes this point by saying, "They are comfortable with their current emotions. Moving forward is challenging, unknown territory in terms of actions and emotion."

Our divorce mediators added that it is not uncommon for one party to retain some hope of salvaging the relationship, while the other party is ready to move on. Thus, a final reason parties may be stuck is that they want to hold on to the past. As mediator Jerry Wood states, "[Parties] want to cling to a relationship that's about to change." For example, ending the marriage by reaching an agreement is often more painful than continuing the conflict, thereby maintaining contact with the other person. Unfortunately, this reality is seldom acknowledged by the reticent party but is relatively easy for experienced mediators to identify. In such cases, parties may be stuck in grief. As mediator Susan Zaidel writes, "The party not happy about ending the marriage often needs more time to digest the reality before he or she will make progress on the assigned tasks, et cetera. It's a delaying tactic, out of emotional need, not a strategic one."

Conflict has become their Life

For some disputants, the conflict feeds their psychological needs in ways that make it difficult to reach resolution and closure. Fighting the good fight may have become a habit or part of their identity. As mediator Douglas E. Noll explains, "The conflict is usually giving meaning or identity to the party." Moreover, some parties come to identify with the conflict in such a way that the dispute becomes entwined with their sense of self. Mediator Alexander Yaroslavsky states the consequences of this phenomenon: "Sometimes people are used to being in a fight and are not ready to let go of that state. I believe that they are energized by the conflict and can get caught up in that paradigm."

On a more complex level, the conflict can become an emergent state. In such cases, a conflict becomes the organizing principle of a party's life, making the resolution of the conflict much harder. As mediator G. Michael Smith explains, "The case or issue has taken on a life of its own and a party sometimes embeds himself in it without truly realizing the grip it has." In these cases, parties cannot move from a past to a future focus without creating a different pattern of interaction and such a transition may be difficult for parties.

Strategies to Move Parties from a Past to a Future Focus

Since mediation is a problem-solving process, its focus is on the future. As a result, when parties are stuck in the past, mediators must help them to look forward. While this can be quite challenging, mediators in our study shared a variety of strategies for helping parties move from a past to a future focus. These tools range from exploring the benefits of moving on to acknowledging parties' pain. In some cases, expert mediators will also conduct reality checks and explain the goal of mediation.

Acknowledge the Parties' Pain

According to our mediators, this strategy involves allowing the parties to vent and share any concerns they have, either in joint session or caucus.

Parties need to be able to share their concerns, fears, perceptions of the problems' causes, and any ideas they have about obstacles to resolution. This can be a time-consuming part of the mediation, but, if unduly rushed, some parties will clam up and refuse to shift from a past to a future focus. Once a party feels heard and understood by the mediator, and hopefully by the other party, she may be more able to move forward with a problem-solving, future-focused discussion.

How Mediators Acknowledge the Parties' Pain

Expert mediators use several strategies to help parties express their pain. A first strategy is to give space for parties to express their feelings and frustrations. Mediators need to listen, summarize what they have heard and, when appropriate, get the other party to also summarize what they have heard or acknowledge the other party's pain. Once each party has felt heard by the mediator and the other party, then it may be easier to transition from a past to a future focus. Mediator Alexander Yaroslavsky explained his strategy: "I allow a lot of time in joint session and/or caucus to give each party as much time as possible to talk about the past, validating their experience. In my experience, once they feel completely downloaded, many feel a release (sometimes they cry; I call it moving from past to present) and make the shift toward the future." While this phase of the mediation process can seem slow, it lays the groundwork for a successful mediation.

While some parties are open and articulate about what is behind their pain or inability to think about the future, others are emotional without necessarily revealing the source of their anxiety or pain. They might say they are overwhelmed and do not know how to cope. Therefore, a second strategy is to explore blaming or a party's resistance to identify what is bothering them. Mediator Douglas E. Noll explores the use of blame: "[I] tease apart the blaming with questions and find out where the deeper emotional components lie. Then I bring those emotions to the surface to be examined." Sometimes, mediators will need to be proactive in helping parties to share and describe their pain. Mediator Sandi Adams explains, "[I] try to uncover any unspoken, unidentified, or unknown concerns or issues still there, acting as an agent of reality about what resolving or not resolving will involve next."

Finally, parties might be reluctant to publicly express what is bothering them. A third strategy is to confront parties. Mediator Madeleine Sauvé explains this strategy: "[I] carry out some individual work with the party, confronting the inconsistencies in their stated goals for the mediation and their behavior and, further to that, an exploration of the underlying sources of the resistance."

When to Acknowledge the Parties' Pain

Not surprisingly, expert mediators acknowledge parties' pain when parties need their pain to be recognized. Expressing one's pain can be done in private caucus or in joint session, depending on a party's need and the reaction of the other party. Often enough, having the chance to explain their pain to the other will be enough for a party to be able to move on. Mediator Alexander Yaroslavsky shares a story that illustrates this strategy:

> A well-established businessman was suing his law firm. Initially he demanded a great deal from the firm. I asked him to explain the history of his demands, which led him to recount the entire story of his relationship with the firm. Once he told the story from start to finish, his view of the conflict changed, as did his demands. He and the firm quickly agreed to a process by which they would determine the calculation of who owed what to whom, and the conflict was largely resolved.

Furthermore, expressing the pain will help parties get some insights into their own behaviors and motivations. Mediator Douglas E. Noll gives an example that illustrates this point:

> A sister blamed brother for taking over after beloved father died. The sister was extremely angry. Conversations led her to understand that her blaming was protecting her from grief, sadness, anxiety, and fear. Once she started processing those deeper emotions, she was able to stop blaming and move constructively in the conflict.

However, in some cases, allowing a party to speak up is not enough. Coaching the other party to be receptive to what is being said will be important. This can be especially true when the other party is not open to the other's pain. Mediator Ericka Gray shares how this strategy can be important:

> A motor vehicle accident victim repeatedly wished to rehash the loss of a particular activity caused by the injuries that he suffered in the accident. The insurance claims adjuster wanted to focus on settlement and didn't want to hear about the impact on the plaintiff's life. Although I listened and asked many questions and learned about how the plaintiff's life had changed, he really wanted the insurance rep to understand. I coached the claims rep about this and the rep was finally able to set aside her bias and spend the time necessary to listen and respond to the plaintiff in a more human-to-human fashion. This allowed the plaintiff to move forward and focus on settlement.

Risks of Acknowledging the Parties' Pain

If done artfully, acknowledging the pain felt by parties is a low-risk strategy. However, it is important to use language that conveys empathy without implying the mediator has taken sides with or against a party. For example, "I can tell this has been upsetting (or difficult for you or sorry for your loss)" versus "I can understand why you are so angry." When poorly framed or executed, it becomes a moderately risky strategy that calls the mediator's neutrality into question. For example, in the event that a party tells a convincing and painful story of loss or violation, it can be genuinely difficult for the mediator to convey empathy without appearing biased toward or against a party. To mitigate this risk, it might be helpful to allow parties to vent in caucus, especially if the mediator is concerned about maintaining the appearance of neutrality.

It is one thing to avoid letting the other party hear you convey empathy that might negatively impact his view of the mediator's neutrality. It is another to actually stay neutral in the face of compelling stories from one or more parties. In a wrongful death suit, a case of medical malpractice, or a divorce with egregious domestic violence, it is important not to discount the events of the past while helping the parties make changes that will meet their future needs. Mediators must remember that maintaining the appearance of neutrality is secondary to actually retaining neutrality. The goal, where appropriate, is to help the parties share their concerns about the past while exploring possible solutions to their dispute.

How can these risks be mitigated? Many books on mediation call for the use of self-reflective practices so that mediators are attentive to their own reactions and feelings within the mediation session. Others talk about focusing on the mediation process and ensuring the mediator has no role in the substance of the case's outcome. Co-mediating may be helpful in highly charged cases, so each mediator has someone to nudge him when he seems to be losing their neutrality and impartiality. However it is done, experienced mediators voiced more concerns about the appearance of neutrality than any actual threats to their neutrality.

Explore the Benefits of Moving On

When parties are focusing on the past, they lose sight of the costs of conflict and the benefits of agreement. Because of this focus, they are not compelled to move on. Therefore, a favorite strategy of expert mediators is to refocus the parties' attention on looking for a solution rather than maintaining a focus on the past. When a mediator helps parties focus on benefits, he tries to motivate them to leave the past behind and move on.

How Expert Mediators Explore the Benefits of Moving On

Expert mediators use various strategies to help parties focus on benefits. The first strategy is to ask parties what they would like to see as an outcome of the mediation. More specifically, mediators may wish to focus the parties on the benefits of finding a solution over the possibility of protracted disputing. Parties often hunger for closure, the ability to put the problem behind them and move on. Mediator Daniel E. Gulden explains his strategy: "[I] show that I understand what has happened and try to get them to picture what they want things to be like in the near future and further out once the conflict is resolved or controlled."

The second strategy is to ask parties about the costs of staying in conflict. The objective is to highlight costs and present mediation as an opportunity to reduce them. Mediator Chris Carlsten outlines her strategy, "I ask them about the impact the continual fighting has had on their lives. I ask them what they would be willing to do to reach a sense of peace and, if there are children, to help their children feel loved, safe, and secure." Some mediators will emphasize the benefits of avoiding the stress of litigation. Mediator Jerome A. Diekemper uses this strategy: "I point out that life after litigation can be much more satisfying and productive than life as a party in a dispute."

In addition to closure and moving on, sometimes mediators ask the parties to think about a post-conflict identity. Therefore, a third strategy is to help parties envision a different future. The objective is to make this alternate path inviting enough to motivate parties to leave the past behind. Mediator Douglas N. Noll explains, "[I] ask the party to envision hypothetical futures, all good. 'What does that future feel, sound, and look like? Would you be willing to explore how to get there from here?' [I] create a different meaning or identity based on peace rather than conflict."

Finally, to be motivated to move on, parties must feel that the benefits are within reach if they move forward. Mediators should thus give parties hope that a positive outcome is possible by offering support and stressing their mediation expertise to parties. As Madeleine Sauvé notes, "People move forward when they can imagine there is something that they can do that will make a difference; when they believe there are resources (the mediator as an example) who will assist them with that plan."

When to Focus on Exploring the Benefits of Moving On

When parties do not want to deal with an issue, expert mediators try to help parties focus on benefits to engage them in problem solving. More specifically, mediators will focus on the benefits of moving on and/or the costs of staying in conflict. Mediator Chris Carlsten offers an example of how highlighting the costs of a conflict can help two parties move forward:

> When I asked one couple about the impact the continual fighting had on them, they each came up with a lot of somatic illnesses they had been suffering. When they were asked about the impact on their children, they said the kids were failing at school, had become withdrawn, and were acting out. Going

> over this helped them to see that there might be a way out of the hell they had created.

Expert mediators also help parties focus on the benefits of when conflict will leave their lives. More specifically, mediators help parties envision a future in which the conflict is not the center of their life. Mediator Douglas E. Noll illustrates how this strategy can be used with a party who is completely invested in a conflict:

> [This case involves] two former business partners in conflict over the sale of a building. One partner wants to fight the good fight. I asked her how this was serving her and that led us into the deeper emotional experience of abandonment, fear, and anxiety. We imagined a life without these feelings and worked through the need to fight the good fight.

Risks of Exploring the Benefits of Moving On

Exploring the benefits of moving on is a low risk situation. Focusing on the benefits of settlement is akin to pointing out the costs of continuing the fight, which is a form of reality checking. If the mediator goes beyond the use of open-ended questions and instead pressures the parties to settle or to accept specific settlement terms, then this becomes ethically dubious and more risky. To reduce this risk, it is advisable to avoid recommending specific settlement terms, but instead highlight the benefits of settlement itself.

Conduct a Reality Check

Sometimes, parties are not realistic about their hopes to maintain the status quo. For example, mediators from the field of family and divorce mediation noted that the unwillingness to shift from a past to a future focus is particularly common in their cases. Generally, one party wants the divorce more strongly than the other or one party feels more betrayed or hurt than the other party. These feelings often leave disputants in denial about the severity of the dispute or the inevitability of its resolution, one way or another. Similarly, workplace mediators often relate examples of parties postponing the negotiation of a severance package with the hope that their employer will offer to take them back. In such cases, expert mediators will double-check parties' unrealistic expectations about holding onto the past.

How Expert Mediators Conduct a Reality Check

Expert mediators use reality checks mainly to remind parties that refusal to address the problem in mediation will not make it go away. The objective is to help parties realize that they will not be able to avoid dealing with the problem. Mediators will also point out to each party that they can either take control of how the conflict will be resolved or let other people decide (and risk not being satisfied). Mediator Edward Blumstein explains this strategy, "[I ask] a lot of questions with the goal of having the party who is not ready to end the conflict accept the reality of the situation. Either they will take charge of the necessary decisions or the court will."

When Focusing on Conducting a Reality Check is Appropriate

The reality check is the preferred strategy of expert mediators when parties do not want to deal with issues. The principle is to stress the inevitability of having to resolve the conflict, and the fact that, as more time passes, the higher the costs will be. An expert mediator illustrated this strategy with one of his cases: "A husband was not ready to be divorced from his wife. Acknowledging this openly and understanding that no fault divorce meant it was an inevitability enabled him to resolve." Furthermore, mediators need to give parties enough time to accept the necessity of moving forward. Mediator Susan Zeidel illustrates how slowing down the process can help a party accept the necessity of turning the page:

> Recently I saw a couple involving a wife who was pushing to work out a divorce agreement while the husband was truly still in shock. He was totally unable to relate to the issue of talking to the children about the divorce or even collecting financial information. After commenting about the huge gap between them, and because the woman still cared about her husband and understood his difficulty, she was able to lower the pressure and agreed to move along at his pace, slow as it may be.

In some cases, mediators will do the reality check to help parties see how their attitude is blocking the resolution of the conflicts. Parties must sometimes realize that their attitude is the real roadblock to resolution. Mediator Jerry Wood gives an example,

> A brother and sister inherited property that one wished to sell and the other wished to keep, but he/she didn't have the money to purchase because he/she received more of the estate. In mediation, each blamed the other for many things that happened to cause the disproportionate allocation of the estate by the parents. In working with the adult siblings, we talked about the dynamics of blame and how it was affecting each other's ability and willingness to resolve the situation.

Risks of Conducting a Reality Check

Reality checks can start out gentle and become increasingly tough as the case and parties' needs indicate. The main risk is that mediators may appear biased as they try to convince parties that it is time to move on. Parties may feel the mediator is trying to pressure them because the other party requested it. However, the risks of reality checks must be balanced against the risks of not conducting a reality check. If the parties are stuck and the risk of impasse is high, then reality checks will probably not make things worse.

There are a number of ways that mediators can mitigate the risks inherent in reality checks. First, by using caucus neither party risks a loss of face in front of the other side. If a mediator asks a party to think through the costs of continuing the conflict, and those costs are not equally shared by all parties, then the party with the highest costs might feel this technique is akin to a case evaluation. If one side is being more recalcitrant than the other, discussing this in caucus may do less damage to his or her bargaining position in the eyes of the other side. In addition to using caucus, the mediator may wish to tell all parties that reality checks will be doled out to each side, so that one party does not get the impression that the mediator is hard on one side only.

Explain the Goal of Mediation

During a mediator's opening statement, he or she usually explains the goals of the process. Mediators will commonly describe the benefits of the process, along with providing a mental map that allows the parties to understand what to expect during the mediation session. However, it is often necessary to re-explain the mediator's role. Whenever a party begins to argue her case to the mediator as if she were a judge, then we know she does not fully understand the role of the mediator as distinct from that of a judge. This behavior indicates the party is seeking to convince the mediator of the rightness of her interpretation of events or positions. When this happens, mediators need to stress that mediation is not about finding who is responsible.

How Expert Mediators Explain the Goal of Mediation

A first strategy is to explain the impartial role of the mediator. More specifically, mediators should point out they have no control over the outcome and their role is limited to shepherding the dispute resolution process. Mediator Susan V. Edwards explains, "I point out that I am not a judge and that the decisions are up to them, not me. So believing that one party has been wronged or one is to blame really isn't going to influence the outcome. Making the other party look bad doesn't make any difference in how I help them address the real issues."

A second strategy is to stress out that mediation is not about finding who is guilty, but about finding a solution. At its heart, this strategy is about explaining the goal of mediation compared with the court process or other routes for dispute resolution. Mediator Daniel E. Gulden says, "[I] help the person understand that blame may not resolve the issue/problem." Mediator Jerry Diekemper agrees, "I suggest that nonadmission clauses are almost uniformly required in settlement agreements and the only way to be declared right is to win at trial and on appeal, which is what our negotiation at the mediation is seeking to avoid."

A third strategy is to help the party see the futility of trying to convince the other that he is guilty. In fact, focusing too much on blame can lengthen the dispute. Mediator Daniel E. Gulden illustrates this point, "[I tell parties that] focusing on fault is not necessary to resolve the dispute and can make it more difficult, time consuming, and costly." Parties should be reminded that mediation is helpful when addressing payment for damages or other future actions, rather than determining past guilt. An expert mediator expands on this point:

> I tell them that it may take a lot of time to try to convince the other party that they should take full responsibility for the problems that led to the divorce, and that might not be the best use of our time in mediation. Sometimes, I even explain the role of psychological denial and how it makes it nearly impossible for us to objectively view our own behaviors. With this information, parties are usually able to put aside the need to convince the other party to take the blame and instead focus their attention on moving forward.

When Explaining the Goal of Mediation is Appropriate

The preferred strategy for dealing with blame-focused parties is to remind them mediation is not about finding guilt. This does not mean that establishing guilt is not important: in a criminal or liability case it may well be important, but mediation is not the best forum for determining guilt as there is no judge nor jury. Parties need to be aware that, although a party may admit guilt in mediation, the mediator has no ability to issue a ruling on guilt. Mediator Ed Blumstein illustrates how this strategy was used in a case:

> Husband blames wife for being a spendthrift and therefore is reluctant to give her the funds to support her lifestyle. I recognize husband's feelings and remind both of them that they did not come to me to be their judge and determine who is right or wrong.

Risks of Explaining the Goal of Mediation

Explaining the collaborative nature of mediation is a low-risk strategy because parties understand the mediator is required to explain the mediation process. Parties are usually able to accept the fact that mediators simply lack the legal or moral authority to issue judgments about who is right or wrong. The main risk for mediators is appearing as if they are trying to downplay parties' concerns. A party may get upset if the mediator says that identifying the guilty party is irrelevant in mediation. This risk can be mitigated by explaining that mediators' opinions do not hold much weight since they are not empowered to make rulings. Mediators may also wish to explain psychological concepts such as denial, which may make it difficult for even the guiltiest parties to objectively evaluate their own culpability. Therefore, spending a great deal of time trying to convince the other side he is the bad guy might not be useful. With this coaching on conflict resolution concepts, parties may be able to better understand the mediator's role.

SUMMARY

When mediations result in impasse, it is often because the parties were unable to move from a past to a future focus. The point at which the mediation turns from a discussion of the past to one of the future is a crucial phase in the mediation process. Mediations that do not reach this step will never result in settlement. Successful, experienced mediators have developed a toolkit for dealing with this common problem, including acknowledging the parties' pain, exploring the benefits of moving, reminding parties that mediation is not a process designed to assign guilt or blame, the use of reality checks about holding on to the past, and explaining the benefits of mediation. By employing these techniques, mediators are generally able to help the parties transition from a discussion of what happened in the past to a problem-solving discussion about what will make the future better for all parties. Table 8.1 below summarizes strategies used by mediators when dealing with parties who are stuck in the past.

Table 8.1. Summary of Strategies to Help Parties Move from Past to Future Focus

STRATEGIES	HOW?	WHEN?	RISK?
Acknowledge the Pain	*- Give space to express the pain* *- Explore criticism* *- Confront parties*	*- Parties want their pain to be recognized*	*- Appear to be taking sides*
Explore the Benefits of Moving On	*- Benefits of moving forward* *- Costs of staying in conflict* *- Think about a post-conflict identity* *- Offer support to move on*	*- Parties do not want to deal with the issues* *- Conflict has become part of parties' lives*	*- Appear to push for concessions*
Conduct a Reality Check	*- Stress that the problem won't go away*	*- Parties don't want to deal with issues*	*- Appear to be taking sides*
Explain the Goal of Mediation	*- Explain mediator's role* *- Explain mediation goal* *- Stress the futility of blaming*	*- Parties want someone to be held responsible*	*- Appear to be downplaying concerns*

Chapter Nine

Dealing with Entrenched Positions

I won't take one penny less!

She needs to apologize first, then we can talk.

He can have joint custody over my dead body!

Statements like this are commonly heard in mediation sessions. It is no surprise that one of the biggest challenges facing mediators is dealing with entrenched positions. Entrenchment has long been linked to impasse (Bennett and Hughes 2005; Beer and Stief 1997) and has given rise to many techniques designed to help uncover the hidden interests that often present themselves as positions (Fisher and Ury 1981). Entrenched positions are often accompanied by a panoply of other mediation banes: refusal to listen to each other, the use of personal attacks or escalatory language, general inflexibility, et cetera.

Entrenchment can take many forms in mediation. One party may feel his position is morally right and that he does not need to compromise. Another party may have *jackpot syndrome* and believe that he will win big in court. From this perspective, settling in mediation would be foolish. These entrenched positions present themselves in a variety of ways, mostly by preventing any form of compromise. In each case, dealing with entrenched positions without alienating the parties may be quite challenging for a mediator.

Some mediated solutions certainly occur through collaborative, expand-the-pie approaches. However, in some cases, both sides must compromise in order to reach a solution that is acceptable to all. Entrenched positions rule out compromise as a possible method of dispute resolution.

Experienced, successful mediators have found ways of dealing with entrenched positions so as to help parties progress, solve problems, and reach resolutions. This chapter will examine the reasons entrenched positions pose such a challenge by breaking down the various root causes of entrenchment. Then we examine strategies used to overcome entrenched positions and share mediator success stories.

WHY PARTIES BECOME ENTRENCHED

We asked mediators to be specific about the reasons why an entrenched position is a hard challenge to overcome. This story from mediator Robert Leitch helps illustrate one of the many reasons why parties get stuck on a specific position or become unwilling to budge:

> I had a mediation—a personal injury case—in which, after making substantial progress, the plaintiff stalled at $100,000 even though his attorney encouraged him to continue reducing his demand. After trying to do more reality checks and discussing the risks, I looked directly at the plaintiff and told him he had every right to insist on whatever amount he thought fair, but that I really wanted to understand why, in light of our discussion and his lawyer's recommendations, he was insistent on accepting no less than $100,000. He looked at me and said, 'That is what the guys at the coffee shop told me it was worth.' And in spite of mine and his lawyer's best efforts and every idea we could borrow from the other side, he didn't budge—at least not on that day.

Expert mediators gave us many reasons why parties may become entrenched. Their answers can be broken down into four roughly equal categories: parties feel morally right; parties have a poor understanding of the mediation process; parties are unprepared or unwilling to hear each other; and parties are not ready to compromise (see Figure 9.1).

Feelings of being Right

Many of our mediators shared insights and stories about people who felt that their position was the right position and that compromising or even listening to the other party would be wrong on principle. In such cases, parties stake out the moral high ground. As mediator Tony Newport reflects, "Right is only one step away from righteousness. Being right is a powerful filter to stop listening." Moreover, as mediator Jerry Wood states, "[Parties are] so emotionally invested in the conflict that being right is more important than reaching a productive resolution."

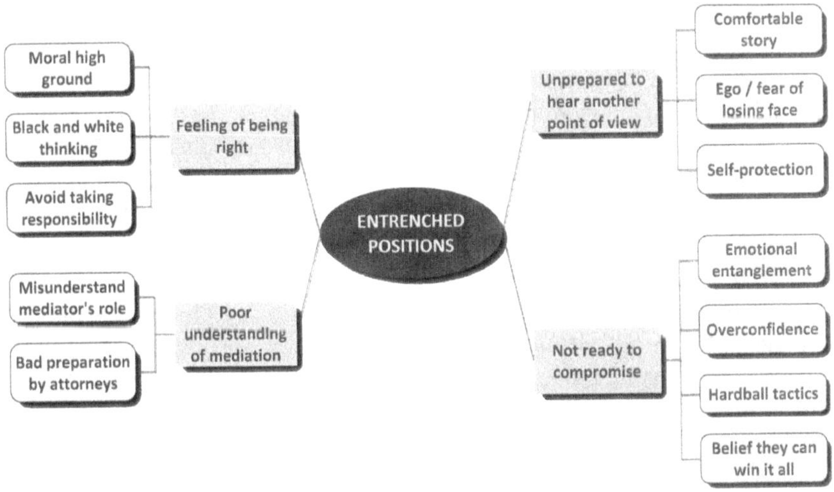

Figure 9.1. Mind map of reasons why parties get into entrenched positions

In addition, according to our mediators, some parties simply are more comfortable with black and white thinking. Disputes between a good guy and bad guy are easier to understand and psychologically less threatening than is the need to acknowledge complexity in people. Mediator Jerry Diekemper elaborates on this point: "People with strong feelings based on morality tend to see any other position than theirs as being unprincipled."

Our mediators indicated that some parties stick to entrenched positions in order to avoid taking any responsibility for the dispute. In such cases, parties want to avoid the negative emotions associated with being somewhat responsible. Acknowledging mutual responsibility for a problem would reduce the feeling of being right and lead to a willingness to compromise or at least listen to the other party. As mediator Vivian Berger mentions, "Clinging to righteousness protects people against feelings of doubt, helps to make them feel justified in a way that reference to self-interest alone cannot."

Poor Understanding of Mediation

A recurring theme underlying many of the challenges to the process is the parties' poor understanding of the mediation process. David Lichter notes, "Parties have unrealistic expectations or misunderstandings of what the system can deliver." Some parties and their attorneys approach mediation the same way they approach arbitration or court. Mediator Don Greenstein reflects, "Sometimes people feel that the mediator is going to make a decision. Once they understand that is not so, usually they can get down to brainstorming."

Parties also have a poor understanding of what to expect. Unfortunately, the media tends to highlight those employment cases in which the employees win at trial much more frequently than those cases in which the employer wins. They also emphasize the large awards that are outliers, leading employees to have jackpot syndrome when they attempt to analyze their own case. This leads to false beliefs among employees about their chances of winning and winning big. According to Neilson and Beim (2004), parties are likely to believe their case has a much better chance of settling than it actually does, and that the award will be up to thirty times higher than statistics predict.

Furthermore, a host of mediator comments focused on the need for attorneys to adequately prepare their parties for mediation, including the need to explain how the process works and the parties' responsibility for reaching agreements in mediation, counteracting any unrealistic expectations. As mediator John E. Sands notes, "[Sometimes] attorneys inflate expectations to get the case and then need the mediator to bring the client down to earth." Researchers also noted that attorneys, union representatives, and other repeat players in the mediation process often do not clearly understand foundational mediation concepts such as integrative bargaining (Fisher and Ury 1981).

Finally, in some cases, parties truly want a judgment rather than a mediation. In those cases, clarifying the limits of the mediator's role is insufficient to meet their needs and impasse is the likely result.

Unprepared to Hear Another Point of View

Sometimes parties maintain entrenched positions because they are unwilling to listen to the other's point of view. As mentioned previously, it is difficult to get parties to really listen to the other side when doing so may result in the need to take some responsibility for the problem or acknowledge the validity of alternative viewpoints. Mediator Doug Thompson writes, "It is often easier to stay attached to a familiar and comfortable story than to really explore what the other parties are thinking and feeling."

Parties may also be reluctant to hear another point of view because of face-saving. As mediator Don Greenstein states, "[Sometimes,] one party's ego is much bigger than the other and they refuse to be seen as being wrong." Furthermore, mediator Vivian Berger writes, "Intransigence can be a self-protective device. Some feel that to entertain any competing idea is tantamount to accepting it and thereby giving up one's own deeply held position." Yet any potential settlement will certainly require parties to listen to each other, either through direct discussions or through the shuttle diplomacy of the mediator.

Not Ready to Compromise

Some parties are simply not ready to entertain the idea of compromise. Of course, not all mediated resolutions require compromise: some result in true win-win options for both parties. Yet fear of compromise keeps many parties from exploring mutually beneficial options in negotiations. First, parties may just not be ready to compromise because of their emotions. Mediator Robert Leitch points out, "Some parties are not yet emotionally ready to settle, and this is a blocking mechanism."

Second, parties may not want to compromise because they are overly self-confident about winning. Mediator Rachel Fishman Green notes, "If they are the kind the person who is always 100% sure of him- or herself, then being open to different ideas in mediation discussion is difficult." In addition, some people are simply gamblers who are not afraid of taking chances with a judge. Some parties may prefer gambling to win big over negotiating a reasonable compromise. As mediator Robert Leitch mentions, "It is usually a matter of their normal risk tolerance or it is because they give greater value to the opinions of their friends and relatives than their own lawyer."

Third, our mediators noted that some parties hold entrenched positions as a hardball negotiation tactic. They believe they will come out with more in the end if they do not agree to compromise. Mediator Don Greenstein observes, "[Some parties] do not want to negotiate with the other side [because] they know what is best for themselves."

Fourth, our commercial mediators also noted the existence of the belief that this lawsuit will make them rich. People hear about a spilled cup of coffee resulting in a settlement worth tens of thousands of dollars and they come to believe that litigation is the path to wealth. As mediator Robert J. McDonnel points out, "In civil matters, the plaintiff sometimes thinks they can get everything including their attorney's fees. Parties also think they should be compensated for their grief and aggravation." In a similar vein, some parties have had their expectations elevated by friends or family members who seek to be supportive by telling the party how he is right and the other party should have to pay for what he has done. Once a party gets an anchoring number stuck in his head, any offers made in mediation can seem paltry and unacceptable, regardless of the likelihood of achieving that number in court.

Finally, parties sometimes have inflated expectations: not about court outcome, but about mediation outcome. In such cases, parties wrongly expect that the other party will simply give up during mediation. In short, they believe that entrenchment will pay off. Mediator Jerome A. Diekemper reflects on this point: "Suggesting to the reluctant party that it is not realistic to expect the other side to unconditionally surrender without a compromise. In legal cases, I can usually get attorneys to admit there is no guarantee of victory. It then follows that some compromise may be advisable."

STRATEGIES FOR ENTRENCHED POSITIONS

Mediators use a number of tools to address the challenge of entrenched positions. These tools include the use of reality checks ranging from subtle to highly assertive or evaluative suggestions. These strategies also include asking the parties to explain why their current position is meeting their needs better than other possible positions; allowing parties to vent their emotions and feel heard; asking parties to envision more positive futures and develop strategies to get there; and even threatening to end mediation. Successful mediators do not give up and declare impasse at the first sign of entrenchment. Instead, they dig into their toolbox of strategies to uncover the sticking points and help the parties to move past them.

Reality Checks

When parties are stuck or nearing impasse for almost any reason, one of the favorite strategies of an experienced mediator is using a reality check. This is a mediation technique that encourages the parties to reassess the certainty of success at trial or rethink the costs of continuing the dispute. A good reality check gets parties to consider the other side's perspective; consider how a neutral person (like a judge) might view the dispute; acknowledge that winning through adjudication is not guaranteed; and consider the costs and benefits of settlement in mediation versus settlement through other venues.

How Mediators Conduct Reality Checks

Expert mediators use various reality check strategies. Firstly, some mediators will help parties consider their odds of winning in court, if that is the likely next venue for the case. For example, mediator Jerome A. Diekemper states, "I also often use gambling metaphors such as flipping a coin, spinning the wheel, rolling the dice, or buying lottery tickets to see how risk averse the party is and to check how realistic they are being." Evaluative mediators may go so far as to share with the parties their own valuation of their case along with their chances of success at trial. Moreover, mediators can explain to plaintiffs the concept of burden of proof. For example, mediator Jerry Wood shares his catchphrase: "I often say that being right is one thing, but proving you are right is another."

Secondly, mediators can play the role of the devil's advocate to help parties evaluate the strengths and weaknesses of their cases. Some mediators will use the Socratic method. Mediator John E. Sands gives an example: "I do my reality checks socratically. I'll start my questions with 'Do I correctly understand that . . . ' I then ask them questions that lead them to the realization that their position is based on wrong information or misunderstanding." Other mediators will play dumb and ask parties to explain their positions with the hope they realize the flaws in their reasoning on their own. An expert mediator elaborates, "In a sincere tone, and with the permission of the other party, I ask 'If you don't mind, to help me understand a bit, could you explain to me exactly how you think you will be receiving the $10 million (or whatever) in this matter?'"

Our mediators talked about using gentle reality checks in joint session, and reserving the tougher questions or comments for private caucus. It is important to remember that asking difficult questions requires parties to think about possibilities they had purposefully been trying to avoid. Some parties do not want to think about how much it will cost to take their case all the way to trial or through an Equal Employment Opportunity Commission (EEOC) investigation. They do not want to think about the possibility that they could lose big or that the case could drag on for years. Forcing parties to think through these possibilities could elicit a fight or flight response, with negative consequences. Mediators may also want to make sure that parties understand that they play devil's advocate with each of them. Mediator Robert N. Leitch describes his approach:

> I try to ask the reality check questions in as neutral a tone and manner as possible. If I get them angry, I apologize and explain to them (usually again) why I am asking these types of questions, assure them I do the same when I go meet with the other side, and rephrase the question if necessary. Fortunately, I am usually backed up by their lawyer.

Thirdly, mediators may explain to parties the cognitive biases that make it difficult for parties to accurately judge the value of their own cases. Research has long shown that individuals are bad at gauging the value of their own cases or accurately predicting their likelihood of success a trial (Goldberg et al. 2007). Mediator David Lichter states, "I discuss litigation statistics. Someone is wrong at least half the time when they go to court, and almost no one goes to trial thinking they will lose."

Finally, it might be necessary to do a reality check on the mediation process itself, when parties think the other will make all the concessions. This happens when parties feel their case is so strong that the other party will give in without a fight. Mediator Jerome A. Diekemper would "suggest to the reluctant party that it is not realistic to expect the other side to surrender unconditionally without some compromise. In legal cases I can usually get attorneys to admit there is no guarantee of victory. It then follows that some compromise might be advisable."

When Conducting Reality Checks is Appropriate

Typically, reality checks are most likely to occur once an impasse has been reached or seems imminent because one or both parties feel they are right. If the mediation is making progress and both sides are displaying flexibility and respect, then reality checks are less necessary. However, when a party is unwilling or unable to engage in a problem solving discussion, then it may be time to break out the reality checks. This story from mediator Jerry Wood helps illustrate how this can be done:

> In a personal injury case, the insurance company made a substantial offer, which the plaintiff immediately rejected. After some discussion, the insurance company made a final offer. In caucus, the plaintiff said that he thought a jury would award more than the offer and wanted to go for it. We went over the case element by element and the total out-of-pocket expenses were far short of the offer made by the insurance company. I said, "Ok, the offer on the table takes care of all your expenses and a good deal more. This is not a maybe offer. It is money in your pocket right now. This is what you have, it is yours. Are you willing to risk this amount that you have against the chance that a jury might award more? Have you considered what this amount of money in your bank account means to you today?"

The key to a successful reality check lies in its timing. Done too early in mediation, it undermines the parties' self-determination by sending a signal that the mediator is not interested in hearing all they have to say or exploring their concerns. Done too late, tempers may have already gotten out of control, making civil discussion and analytical thinking difficult.

Sometimes, the reality check will not be about the chances of winning it all, but about the practicality of an entrenched position. In some cases, parties may stick to a position that does not make sense or is not realistic. In such cases, the mediator should help the entrenched party assess the implications of his position. An expert mediator relates a story that illustrates this strategy:

> [In a mediation, the] father refused to have a home phone, get a cell phone, or reveal his postal address to the mother. He knew he was right and never, ever, ever would have anything to say to the mother. He claimed the kids never complained about being with their dad. He showed up ready to leave. I opened a discussion about whether, in theory, if a grandparent died, it would be good or bad to locate the kids and get a message to them so they could attend the funeral. I had already gathered that both parties had great respect and trust for both sets of grandparents. As we talked about it and statutory requirements for medical and other emergency contact mediation, the father sort of chuckled about his strident position and loosened up considerably. Eventually, both sides set up contacts through a neighbor and the father agreed to get cell phones for himself and each child.

Risks of Conducting Reality Checks

According to the mediators in our study, the risks of reality checks range from low to high. These risks vary with the strength of the reality check. A reality check that is too strong or that pushes too hard against a party's urge for denial or their preferred view of the dispute can land like a lead balloon. In the worst-case scenario, a party might storm out of the mediation, ending the process. In other situations, parties can interpret reality checks as a sign of mediator partiality or a loss of the mediator's neutrality. To avoid this, it is helpful to remind the parties that you will be asking difficult questions of all parties, not just one side. One mediator stated that she tries to make it clear that when she asks difficult questions of one party, she will do the same to the other party, too. Some mediators remind the parties that it is their job to play devil's advocate or to get the party to think about how a judge or jury might view the evidence or the other side's perspectives.

Before employing a reality check, it is helpful to build up some positive rapport with the parties by acting as a good listener during opening statements and by modeling respectful and impartial body language and behaviors throughout the mediation session. The mediator's opening statement is also a time when the mediator can briefly convey his or her qualifications and experience so that the parties believe the mediator is knowledgeable about their type of case. However, when mediators boast at length about their own qualifications, ironically, it has a contrary effect and reduces the parties' trust in the mediator, as it appears as bragging (Stimec and Poitras 2009).

Have Parties Explain their Positions

When parties are entrenched, they often do not want to hear the other's point of view. Unless information is shared, the mediator and parties cannot get at the interests that underlie the positions (Fisher and Ury 1981). Mediators in these situations need to encourage parties to listen and understand the other's point of view. Often enough, parties will discover how to move away from their entrenched positions when they realize that they are not that far apart, or that the other's motives are not as unjustified as they initially thought.

How Mediators Ask Parties to Explain their Positions

Expert mediators use several strategies to have parties listen to the other's position. Firstly, a number of mediators mentioned the importance of using their opening statement to convey to the parties that the mediation process requires mutual listening and respect in order to succeed. Mediator Tony Newport explains, "I name up front that they must listen to each other as part of the process. I model this behavior and if in the end they refuse to listen, I stop the process."

Secondly, to get the parties to listen and acknowledge each other's perspectives, it is often necessary to remind them that listening to or acknowledging other perspectives is not the same thing as agreeing with the other party. For example, mediator Doug Thompson states, "Often I will reassure parties they do not have to reach a settlement, much less agree with one another about the issues in the dispute. We try to separate listening to understand from evaluating what you think about it."

Thirdly, when parties believe their position is the morally right position, it can be especially difficult to get them to listen to other points of view. In such cases, another strategy is to encourage parties to take a wider outlook. Sometimes it is helpful to get the parties to think about their relationship more broadly, rather than simply focusing on the event that precipitated mediation. Mediator John Ford gives an example of this strategy: "There was a cubicle outburst that was dealt with by a letter of warning. In the post-investigation mediation, the victim was stuck in being right. I said, 'Yes, in respect to this incident you are right. But what about the relationship as a whole?'"

Fourthly, when one party believes that she is right, then she might also believe the other party is lying. Therefore, another strategy is to remind parties that people in conflict with one another usually have genuinely different, even contradictory, memories of events (Beer and Stief 1997). Mediator Vivian Berger explains her strategy as, "I stress that putting an idea out there isn't the same as accepting it, that one can always simply say no."

When Asking Parties to Explain their Positions is Appropriate

Encouraging parties to listen to the other's position is useful when one party feels he is right. Parties should be asked to share more information about their positions when it is not clear where a position came from or what needs it meets. This information needs to be shared with the mediator and all parties. Mediator Don Greenstein gives an example of how forcing parties to listen to each other helps them move beyond entrenched positions:

> A religious leader refused to change a religious practice that caused others in a community to be bothered by the practice. With an explanation of why the behavior was important, there was a give and take on both sides.

When parties are unprepared to hear the other's story, encouraging parties to listen to each other is also useful. Once parties have heard each other's needs and interests, rather than only their positions, they are often able to come up with their own potential solutions to the dispute. If not, they at least leave the process with a fuller understanding of the other's concerns and worldviews. Mediator Douglas E. Noll relates a story that illustrates how hearing the other point of view can break impasse:

> It was a congregational dispute involving the typical old liturgy/new liturgy conflict. In this case, the parties were extremely polarized and escalated. The trick was to discuss why any liturgy was important and how it fit into the lives of the disputants. That led to some heartfelt revelations and mutual respect.

Risks of Asking Parties to Explain their Positions

Having parties listen to the other's interests is a low-risk strategy overall. In fact, this strategy generally amounts to no more than the routine information gathering that parties expect from the mediator. But no strategy is completely risk free. Depending on how the question is framed, parties may take the mediator's questions as a sign that he wants to force parties to accept the other's position or they may feel a need to defend their position.

The most common risk with this strategy is that the parties frame their explanations of their positions in ways that cast blame on the other party or otherwise escalate the conflict. Again, the judicious use of caucus will reduce any risk posed by this strategy. The risk is low when emotions are low and parties seem to be behaving in a civil manner toward one another.

Help Parties Evaluate the Costs of Conflict

People have a tendency to focus on the potential gains or even windfalls that might come from a trial or courtroom outcome (Lewicki et al. 2009). Frequently, parties do not think about the potential for loss. A key mediation opportunity might be to help parties reframe how they estimate the costs of losing or maintaining the conflict. In fact, sometimes winning can be quite costly.

How Mediators Help Parties Evaluate the Costs

Expert mediators use various strategies to help parties assess the cost of a conflict. Firstly, mediators may ask parties and attorneys to evaluate the costs of continuing the conflict not only in terms of money, but also emotional costs and time. For example, mediator Robert Leitch states, "[I] discuss what the actual result at trial would have to be to net the amount that would come out of the offered settlement today. [I] include not only the monetary award, but time, stress, out-of-pocket costs, and other nonmonetary factors. [We] talk about how satisfying or unsatisfying the end result will be even if the judge or jury says they are right. I very directly ask them if it is worth it."

Attorneys generally have the greatest ability to accurately estimate the costs of continuing on to adjudication, as well as the likely timeline and steps necessary in that process (i.e., depositions, further testing, or investigation, et cetera). If parties are unrepresented, the mediator can walk them through a series of questions designed to make them think about the steps necessary to continue with the dispute, as well as the timeline for resolution through a formal process such as adjudication.

In addition, parties sometimes need the help of the mediator to sift through all of the possible outcomes if the case proceeds without settlement in mediation. Mediator Jerry Wood says, "People tend to be risk takers [for] gain, but [are] risk averse as to losses. I change perspectives so that the parties see both sides. If the party is focusing on possible gains, I focus on possible losses."

Secondly, mediators may ask parties to evaluate the opportunity costs related to prolonging the dispute's lifecycle. For example, some mediators ask: "How much time and money have you spent on this case so far? How much are you willing to spend?" If the parties will have an ongoing relationship, such as coworkers, co-parents, neighbors, landlord-tenants, etc., then it is important to examine the emotional and practical costs of ongoing conflict as well. It might also be that the parties have other problems or projects to take care of that are more valuable than the ongoing dispute.

When Helping Parties Evaluate the Costs is Appropriate

This strategy is mostly appropriate when parties feel they are right and they do not mind incurring some costs to prove it. Additionally, this specific kind of reality check is useful when a party or attorney seems nonchalant about proceeding through the litigation process to adjudication. Even if one side believes it has a 100 percent chance of winning at trial, the party may reconsider the benefits of mediation when he fully considers the resources it will take to get to trial—including time, money, and emotional energy. A expert mediator gives us an example of how a mediator can help parties assess the cost of maintaining a conflict:

> In a workplace dispute based on gender discrimination, during private caucus, I asked each side to consider what would happen in the event they didn't settle. Because the complainant faced a more challenging situation, I asked the complainant's counsel to fully explain the financial, time, and emotional costs of not reaching an agreement.

Risks of Helping Parties Evaluate the Costs

This strategy is not without risks. Mediators run some risk of alienating attorneys, who may prefer to take the case to trial or feel the mediator is improperly influencing their clients. Most attorneys are willing to provide estimates of the costs of going all the way with the case. Yet some attorneys will simply not play along and will not give a range of potential costs of litigation; nor will they hazard a guess at how long it may take to resolve the case, either through settlement outside of mediation or through adjudication.

Furthermore, bringing up these transaction costs may make attorneys uncomfortable by forcing parties to weigh the benefits of having their day in court versus quicker and cheaper closure.

Mediators can mitigate this risk by privately asking attorneys if they are comfortable with this line of questioning. This also raises a potential dilemma: what if the party wants to think this through, but the attorney does not? In the end, mediators are there for the parties, but it is foolish not to at least acknowledge the potential risk of alienating attorneys. This may raise serious ethical dilemmas in jurisdictions or case streams in which the attorneys choose the mediators. Since this is usually done in caucus, another way to mitigate these risks is to clarify that you will be asking these questions of both sides.

Envision a Better Future

Some mediators also mentioned using a positive technique in which they invited the parties to think about better future outcomes, positive ways forward, or ideal futures. The objective is to motivate parties to shift away from entrenched positions. This strategy could more aptly be described as envisioning. For example, mediator John E. Sands states, "Give the claimant another dream. Or another way of getting on with life." Since parties with entrenched positions are focused on past wrongs, hurts, and narratives of themselves as the victim or the right person, getting them to think about the future instead is difficult, but powerful.

How Mediators Help Parties Envision a Better Future

Expert mediators use several strategies to help parties envision a better future. Firstly, it can be helpful to get the parties to engage in brainstorming or to think broadly about all types of possible outcomes by suggesting possibilities they had not considered. Mediator Georgia Geiger reports the following example: "Mom has decided on a specific amount of child support because that is what her neighbor receives. Ask her if she would accept a larger amount—brainstorm about how that could happen in order to get the brainstorming started."

Secondly, it is helpful for mediators to be metacognitive about the brainstorming phase of mediation. This means that mediators take a moment to explain to parties the techniques they are using and why they have chosen these techniques. For example, an expert mediator might say, "I would like us to spend some time brainstorming all the various ways to make the future better than the past. I will encourage you to refrain from evaluating any ideas until all possible ideas have been listed on the board. Don't hold any ideas back—you never know what ideas may hold the seeds of resolution."

Thirdly, if parties seem shy or hesitant to throw out ideas, the mediator could throw out one or two outlandish ideas, just to get them talking. For example, in most disputes there is the option of litigation or dropping the case. All or nothing solutions are generally not acceptable to either party, but they get the discussion started, so long as the mediator makes it clear that these are extreme examples, not the mediator's preferred outcomes.

When Helping Parties Envision a Better Future is Appropriate

When parties are stuck in a cycle of blame casting or rehashing the wrongs perpetrated by the other party, envisioning a different future can offer a way out. It is worth noting that the better future can be one in which a benefit is attained or a catastrophe is avoided. Mediator Rachel Fishman Green relates a case in which this strategy helped a party move beyond an entrenched position:

> A parent who felt she was right told a story during mediation of a friend of hers who had been interviewed by a judge when she was 5, during her parents' divorce, and still, at the age of 50, remembers the trauma of going through that. This parent believes heartily that she is right and her ex is wrong, but she also sees the value in settling in mediation, rather than a lengthy trial to fight in the hopes of proving her ex wrong in a public forum.

In addition, envisioning a better future can be about helping parties consider a different way to be compensated. Stock options, future contracts for shared business, getting a job back, and changes in policies or behaviors are all non-monetary methods of compensation. Mediator Jerry Wood shares a wonderful story that illustrates this strategy:

> One party wanted a specific cash amount and not one cent less. The other party admitted some liability, but did not have the ability to pay the amount claimed, and thought the amount exorbitant. In caucus with the first party, I asked how she came up with the amount in controversy. There were a few specific values, but most was compensation of intangible things such as inconvenience, emotional distress, and breach of trust. After a discussion about each of those elements, we talked about how those issues could be addressed in other ways. After taking these concerns to the other party, also in caucus, we reconvened jointly with the second party acknowledging that her actions had caused the first party considerable inconvenience and distress, and she offered to make it right to the best of her ability. The discussion opened up, a resolution was reached, and the two were engaged in conversation as they left.

If the parties express nihilistic sentiments (such as a better future is impossible) or they are overwhelmed with their emotional reactions to the situation, then it may be an indicator of depression, a belief that the party has no power or agency, or otherwise indicate that mediation may not be sufficient to solve the dispute. In these cases, any agreement reached could be overturned later on the grounds that the party was not competent to enter into any agreement. Although rare, it is worth noting. In these cases, declaring an impasse is better than reaching an agreement with a party who lacks the capacity to make good decisions for himself.

Risks of Helping Parties Envision a Better Future

Envisioning a better future is a very low-risk strategy. Most parties are able to envision a better future and work backwards to brainstorm ways to achieve that future. Additionally, parties are generally able to brainstorm so long as they understand that they are not committing themselves to any particular outcome that arises out of the brainstorming process. This strategy does not bring into question the mediator's neutrality, so long as he or she asks each party to engage equally in this exercise.

However, one risk is setting parties' expectations too high. Some parties may get carried away, envisioning an idyllic future, but most understand the hard work that it takes to reach that future. If the mediator is concerned about raising the parties' expectations too high, then he or she can ask the parties to focus on the ways in which they themselves would need to make changes in order to achieve that ideal future, rather than focusing on the changes the other party would need to make.

Threaten to End Mediation

One of the most frequently proposed strategies is to threaten to end mediation with no agreement. If a party is simply sticking to an entrenched position out of a desire to be a hard-nosed negotiator, then this could be the only strategy that will trigger any shift in their position. For example, mediator Don Greenstein states, "I let go and if there is not a give and take, then I let self-determination rule the day." On the other hand, parties have the right to use their self-determination to leave mediation with no agreement. If a party truly wants to be vindicated in a court of law or other authoritative forum, that is her right.

How Mediators Threaten to End Mediation

Mediators in our sample displayed different tolerance levels for game playing on the part of the parties, with some mediators claiming to use the "threatening to end mediation" strategy as a last resort, while others spent less time trying to push intransigent parties toward agreement. For example, mediator John E. Sands says, "I remind them they're paying me and that rigidity is adding to the transaction costs." Nevertheless, expert mediators will usually give parties some time to reconsider their positions before terminating mediation. Mediator Tony Newport explains his strategy:

> I will give people time (up to a week or more) to rethink their position. I will encourage as much support and in some instances organize such support (counseling, mentoring, coaching, union support), and I will invite these support persons into the mediation if appropriate, but I won't persist forever. All parties need to take some responsibility for moving forward.

When Threatening to End Mediation is Appropriate

Mediators can threaten to end mediation when parties do not fully understand that mediation is a give-and-take process, or when parties do not want to negotiate, and little or no movement is forthcoming, even after repeated attempts by the mediator and/or the other parties to evoke movement. When parties remain entrenched in their positions or they articulate a preference for adjudication, an impasse is sometimes unavoidable. Mediator Tony Newport explains his rule of thumb: "I work hard at the front end to ensure that all parties understand the process and I get them signed up to a premediation agreement. If one party then wants to continue to play games, I stop and will probably abandon the process." On the other hand, parties might be right that an issue cannot be negotiated. For example, when concerns about addiction lead a parent to contest visitation by the addicted parent, then agreement in mediation is unlikely.

In some cases, parties do understand mediation, but are unwilling to compromise because they want to play hardball. If the mediator has attempted to brainstorm with the parties, has addressed all issues on which there is disagreement in search of at least a partial agreement, and there is still no movement from the parties, then it is time to threaten to end to the mediation. The key is not to use this strategy too early on in a mediation session. Inexperienced mediators tend to declare impasse much earlier than experienced mediators.

Before declaring impasse, mediators may wish to caucus one last time with each party to ensure that no issues, interests, or options have been left uncovered in joint session. Information shared in these caucus sessions may reinvigorate the discussion. In the end, if a party prefers not to settle in mediation, then he or she has the right to self-determination and mediation should be terminated. Clearly, there are some cases that do indeed need to be settled outside of mediation (e.g., a precedent-setting legal matter, an issue that benefits from public scrutiny, times when one party may have an incentive to stall resolution, the rights of a third party may be impacted negatively or need protection, et cetera).

Risks of Threatening to End Mediation

Obviously, threatening to end mediation is a high-risk strategy. Mediators need to avoid empty threats to end mediation. If parties were ordered to attend mediation, ending the process without an agreement may be their preferred outcome. Therefore, timing is important. Mediators should not threaten to end mediation too early, as parties may not be sufficiently engaged in the process to fully consider the costs of ending mediation. Another risk is not leaving enough time for parties to fully consider the implications of terminating mediation. On the spur of the moment, parties may be inclined to stick to their positions and stop the process, but they may regret it later. To mitigate this risk, mediators should leave some time to reflect and ask questions to help parties consider the implications of ending mediation.

Thus, prior to ending mediation, the neutral mediator should first ask the parties one or more of these questions: What would be the benefits of reaching settlement today versus at a later time or in court? Are there any ideas or proposals we have overlooked? Will you and the other party/parties continue your (working, neighborly, co-parenting) relationship after mediation and even after a court decision in this matter? Or imagine your life five years from now. The dispute has been resolved to your satisfaction and it is behind you. What advice would you give your current self to get this resolved?

SUMMARY

Entrenched positions arise for many reasons: a feeling of being morally right, an unwillingness to listen to the other side, denial of one's own role in the dispute, et cetera. Successful mediators have developed numerous techniques to help parties move away from their positions and explore a host of options that might better meet their needs and result in the settlement of the dispute. These include getting parties to discuss the interests that underlie their positions, playing devil's advocate by asking a party to consider the weaknesses in their own case or see it from the other's perspective, discussing the costs of continued conflict, or even threatening to end mediation with no agreement when parties refuse to get unstuck. Table 9.1 below summarizes how experienced mediators deal with entrenched positions.

Table 9.1. Summary of Strategies to Deal with Entrenched Positions

STRATEGIES	HOW?	WHEN?	RISK?
Reality Checks	*- Assess the odds of winning* *- Play devil's advocate* *- Explain cognitive bias*	*- Feeling of being right*	*- Loss of neutrality* *- Parties may lose face*
Have Parties Explain their Positions	*- Modeling listening* *- Separate listening from deciding* *- Broaden perspectives*	*- Feeling of being right* *- Unprepared to hear another point of view*	*- Confirm the legitimacy of parties' positions*
Help Parties Evaluate the Costs of Conflict	*- Focus on costs* *- Focus on opportunity costs*	*- Unwillingness to compromise*	*- Alienate parties* *- Alienate parties' attorneys*
Envision a Better Future	*- Broaden perspectives* *- Brainstorm ideas* *- Suggestions to keep the ball rolling*	*- Feeling of being right* *- Poor understanding of mediation*	*- Parties unable to be creative*
Threaten to End Mediation	*- Evaluate the suitability of mediation* *- Explain the consequences of ending mediation*	*- Poor understanding of mediation* *- Unwillingness to compromise*	*- Unnecessary end of mediation*

Conclusion

How Do Expert Mediators Mediate?

The chapters in this book have explored the challenges faced during the mediation process. Each chapter examined the reasons why a challenge can lead to impasse; the strategies used by mediators to address the challenge; when and how to use those strategies; and the risks of each strategy. In contrast, this chapter will assess the challenges and strategies together in order to reach a more coherent conclusion about the habits and choices made by expert mediators. In the end, we hope to answer the question: what makes an expert mediator?

Our conclusions fall into two broad categories. First, expert mediators use a multitude of contingent strategies in mediation. Expert mediators cannot easily be labeled as evaluative, facilitative, or transformative in their styles or approaches. Instead, expert mediators use a plurality of mediation models and problem-solving strategies, and their preferred strategy is dependent upon the particular challenge or challenges they face. Second, successful, experienced mediators have one key strategy in common which supports nearly all others: they explore parties' expectations and interests deeply. Upon learning more about parties' needs, expert mediators then choose the specific strategies best suited to meet them.

Overall, we have learned that expert mediators adapt their approaches and consciously choose their strategies to match the needs of the case and the parties, rather than remaining ideologically attached to one mediation style or one set of strategies, irrespective of the idiosyncratic nature of each case.

Thus, expert mediators use contingent strategies and explore parties' expectations and needs to choose the appropriate intervention.

EXPERT MEDIATORS USE CONTINGENT STRATEGIES

One highly robust finding of our study is that expert mediators are adaptive, flexible, intuitive, and pragmatic in their choice of mediation strategy and mediator style. Rather than having only a few tools in their toolbox, they have a plethora of tools at the ready and can use them as needed or not at all.

PLURALITY OF MEDIATION MODELS AND STRATEGIES

Mediation literature is full of debates as to the best style of mediation. Some argue that mediators should stick to interest-based, facilitative styles of mediation, in which the neutral leads the parties through a step-by-step process of information sharing, brainstorming, and problem solving, but always refrains from offering his own opinion or evaluating the strengths and weaknesses of each party's case. This style is commonly labeled facilitative mediation and has been the most commonly taught model in North America. All mediators start mediations this way. However, upon learning more about the various needs of the parties and the previous obstacles to settlement, expert mediators may or may not retain this style throughout the mediation.

The mediators in our study indicated that some cases require a stronger hand from the mediator. Sometimes mediators veer from the facilitative mediation path and use strategies more commonly associated with styles labeled as evaluative, directive, or pressing. These strategies may include the mediator offering an evaluation as to how the case will fare in court or in front of a jury. Short of that, mediators may use strong reality checks to ask parties, "If you were the judge, what would you think about the evidence presented by the other side?" Mediators using this style and its related strategies are more likely to ask the parties to think about the costs and risks associated with moving forward with their case if mediation reaches an impasse. They may praise compromise as a fair and efficient way to reach agreements. They may point out the weak spots in a party's case and ask them to look at their case with fresh eyes, the way a neutral third party might see it. When parties are having difficulty overcoming entrenched positions, strong emotions, or moving from a past to a future focus, some mediators may see these strategies as necessary.

Similarly, our mediators noted that some of the challenges that arise in mediation are ripe for an approach that focuses on the root causes of problems. Usually this means addressing relationship challenges. Mediators who focus on improving the relationship between parties are often called transformative mediators or described as having a narrative approach, which asks parties to fully tell their story and listen to the story told by the other party. When parties will continue to have a relationship after mediation, it makes sense to help them address the sources of stress, miscommunication, or skill deficits that may worsen the current dispute and increase the likelihood of future problems. For divorcing parents, coworkers in an employment dispute, neighbors, or teachers and parents in a special education case, it makes sense to rebuild trust and empower parties to proactively improve their conflict resolution skills and abilities through a focus on relationship building. Our mediators noted that some cases call for a relational approach to mediation while, in others, it is just business and no future relationship will exist.

While academics and practitioners have often argued for the primacy of the facilitative, evaluative, or transformative approach to mediation, our study concludes that expert mediators are not dogmatic in their choice of approach. Within one mediation session, the mediator may use all three styles as the case evolves and knowledge about the parties' needs becomes clearer. The mediators in our study revealed a total of thirty-eight strategies used to overcome the challenges faced in mediation. Expert mediators thus have a large toolbox of mediation strategies.

PREFERRED STRATEGIES DEPEND ON THE SOURCE OF THE CHALLENGE

If we look at the individual mediators who answered questions on each challenge, we find a wide variety of strategies and approaches, as well as stories, to support the ways in which those strategies have been employed to address specific cases. For each of the main challenges arising during the mediation process, expert mediators call on approximately 4.7 different strategies. Depending on the source of a challenge, a different strategy will be used.

Expert mediators encounter a host of challenges and customize their selection and use of strategies accordingly. A party who is highly emotional may need the mediator to use the strategies of listening, caucus, and coaching. A party who is entrenched in his position may need reality checks, help to envision a future without the conflict, or assistance with evaluating the costs and benefits of settlement in mediation. An overly strong reality check might coerce a meek party to accept a settlement that undermines self-determination, while it would not run the same risk with an assertive party. Mediators must calibrate their choice of strategy, as well as the tone in which they employ many of these strategies, to match the needs of the parties, attorneys (when applicable), and the case at hand. Mediators who are only adept at using one style or one set of strategies will be called on for only one type of case, if at all. Thus, expert mediators are adaptive and can handle any case type.

EXPLORING PARTIES' EXPECTATIONS AS A KEY STRATEGY

While most of the techniques mentioned by the mediators in our study were unique to the specific challenge at hand, there was one overarching strategy that was fundamental to the selection of all others: mediators begin by exploring the parties' expectations and needs so as to be able to select the most appropriate path forward and make efficient use of other strategies. The predominant strategy used by expert mediators is to first explore parties' expectations and needs, then choose a more specific strategy to meet those expectations and needs. As the mind map below shows (Figure 10.1), mediators need to explore parties' expectations to build trust in the process, test the validity of expectations, and to reframe their expectations in the service of resolution.

Build Procedural Trust

When mediators are faced with nearly any challenge in mediation, the first thing they do is explore the parties' expectations and learn more about their needs. When concerns are about the mediation process and mistrust between parties, mediators need to build trust procedural trust. For example, when faced with a party who does not want to mediate, the neutral invites the party to share information as to why they feel this way. It may indeed be the fact that the case should not be mediated: perhaps the parties are seeking to set a judicial precedent or there is ongoing violence and coercion that makes mediation inappropriate. Alternatively, the mediator may learn that the parties saw mediation on TV and have an incorrect understanding of the mediator's role or of the process itself. In this case, the mediator's strategy would be to educate the parties about the mediation process. The goal would be to make parties more knowledgeable and comfortable with the mediation process and remind them that agreements will only be reached with their consent.

In another example, a party may be unwilling to reach an agreement with the other party out of a belief that the party will not uphold any agreement reached in mediation. The previous history of action or inaction between the parties is usually to blame for this type of distrust, but there could be other reasons rooted in differing identities, stereotypes, or a simple lack of relational rapport. When distrust gets in the way of reaching an agreement, the mediators in our study say they spend time exploring the concerns and needs of the distrustful party in order to get to the root cause of the problem. Once the root cause is uncovered, then mediators choose additional strategies as appropriate. When seeking to build trust in agreements, mediators generally

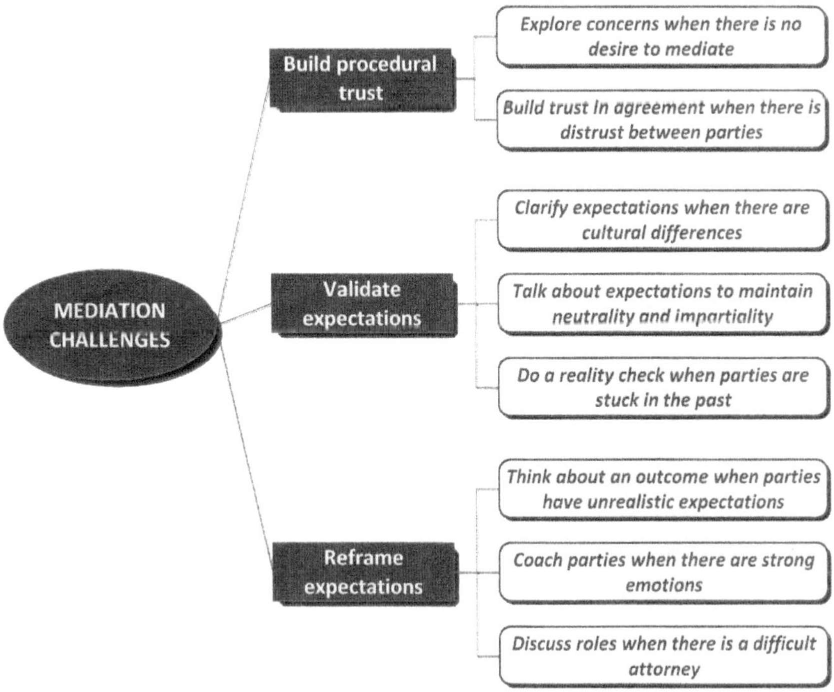

Figure 9.2. Generic strategies to deal with mediation challenges

turn to the use of procedures within the agreement itself. As the chapter on overcoming distrust discussed, this means mediators seek to help the parties craft agreements that include provisions or penalties for default by either party and draft the agreements in ways that incentivize cooperation from all sides.

Validate Expectations

When mediators explore parties' expectations, they may reach the conclusion that one or more parties have a false or incorrect view of the process, the other parties, or the possible outcomes. Parties' expectations may be unrealistic for a number of reasons. For example, a party may be stuck in the past and unable or unwilling to look ahead to how the case may fare in court or drag on without resolution. Parties may not fully understand the role of the mediator or they may have cultural differences that lead to vastly different valuations of the case or expectations of each other's future behaviors. If parties' expectations are based on inaccurate information or misattributions, mediators can then move forward in various ways to address these barriers to resolution.

For example, when a party is stuck in the past, he is likely to predict all future behaviors based on the past behaviors of the other party. However, the formalization of the dispute or some other factor may have precipitated a change in one or more parties that will make the future path of the conflict shift. For example, a workaholic father who has spent little time with his kids may have an epiphany when his spouse files for divorce and he realizes he must change his ways. When he articulates his desire to have more parenting time, his spouse may see this as a ploy to reduce child support rather than a reflection of the changes he has undergone. Mediators may need to encourage parties to test the validity of their expectations by listening to each other and asking each other the tough questions necessary to understand why someone is asking for X, Y, or Z. Reality checks may be needed to help a party move from a focus on the past to a focus on the future.

Parties frequently misunderstand the mediator's role and view her as a judge instead of a neutral party who lacks decision-making authority. A party may believe it is the mediator's role to decide who transgressed in the past, thereby determining moral or legal guilt in a case. A party may believe the mediator has the power to force a preferred outcome. When this happens, mediators usually educate the parties and explain the importance of mediator neutrality and impartiality in terms of the outcome of the case. They explain their role in furthering settlement, as well as their lack of power to force one on the parties. Mediators are expected to provide information about their role and the mediation process, thereby educating the parties as to the purpose and limits of mediation. This is a generally benign task that runs few risks of angering parties or raising concerns about the neutrality or impartiality of the mediator.

When the mediator explores the party's expectations about the outcome of the case, the mediator may reach the conclusion that a party has jackpot syndrome, for example, believing that a minor car accident will be a ticket to riches in the form of a massive settlement payout. Sometimes mediators choose to confront unrealistic expectations (e.g., jackpot syndrome, certainty of prevailing in court, or being stuck in the past) by using stronger reality checks or even offering their own evaluation of the strengths and weaknesses of a case, although the former strategy was mentioned relatively rarely by the mediators in our study. Sometimes a party's expectations about the case are based on attributions about the other side's motivations or expected future actions. When this happens, mediators can ask questions that help uncover and share information about each side's motivations and behaviors in ways that may change the expectations of one or both sides.

A family mediator may explore the expectations of a father from a different region of the world when he says he is 100 percent certain he will be awarded full custody of his young children even though both parents seem to be good parents. If cultural difference is at the root of a party's expectations, it may be helpful for the mediator to explore that issue with the parties. Mediators often encourage parties to seek legal advice or consultation from someone who is bicultural and can explain the differences between U.S. legal systems and the cultural norms that may be the root of the dispute. Inviting each side to share the basis for their expectations can be a helpful exercise for the mediator as well as the parties.

Reframe Expectations

When parties have unrealistic expectations, it can be helpful to play devil's advocate, meaning the mediator asks the parties to consider the other side's perspectives or look more closely at the weaknesses in their own case. The objective is to help parties better adapt their expectations to reality or to what can be successfully negotiated. When an ongoing relationship is at stake, sometimes mediators ask parties to weigh the value of improving that relationship against the need to push for a punitive outcome. Parties may be unrealistic about the outcome of their case if settlement is achieved external to mediation, but they may also have unrealistic expectations about the length of time it will take to achieve their desired outcome and the transaction costs necessary to get them to that outcome. By addressing these expectations directly, mediators can help parties realistically reframe their expectations.

Strong emotions sometimes keep parties from having realistic expectations about their case. For example, one party may think: "After what that hospital did, I want to drive them into bankruptcy!" Mediators can use their coaching skills to work with parties in a caucus session. Sometimes mediators coach the parties on their communication skills, including listening or framing. Sometimes mediators coach parties to reach a better understanding of cultural differences or cognitive biases that may be negatively impacting expectations. Coaching can be used to help parties manage their emotions and understand the ways in which emotions can serve to either hinder or promote their own interests.

Attorneys can provide needed information, case evaluations, and reality checks for their own clients in mediation. However, attorneys and their clients occasionally have different incentives for settlement and different views about the strengths and weaknesses of the case. Mediators often work with parties and their attorneys to clarify expectations, share information, and then reframe expectations in order to reach a shared understanding of the best path forward. Occasionally, mediators are called upon in caucus to improve the communication and understanding between a party and his or her attorney. Sometimes mediators have difficulty learning more about the party's expectations or needs because the attorney discourages the party from speaking. When this happens, mediators often seek to gently and tactfully educate the attorney about the benefits of direct party participation in mediation. Once accomplished, it becomes easier to help the parties reframe unproductive positions into a constructive framing of interests.

SUMMARY

A novice mediator is likely to have been trained to adopt and maintain one specific style throughout the mediation while employing a couple of tricks of the trade, such as the frequent use of caucus and reality checks, when faced with any challenge. In contrast, the defining characteristic of an expert mediator is that he or she thoughtfully chooses between styles and strategies as needed to address the challenges arising in individual mediations and for every unique individual met in mediation. This finding helps to explain previous studies that noted mediators' tendency to claim to prefer one style over another, even though the specific strategies and communicative behaviors chosen within mediation actually vary depending upon the needs of the case at hand (Charkoudian et al. 2010; Wall and Chan-Serafin 2009).

The research conducted for this text leads us to a deeper understanding of the many strategies and approaches used by mediators when faced with the challenges commonly faced in mediation, also known as the primary causes of impasse. While we matched the challenges of the mediation process to the strategies used by experienced mediators, one limitation of this study is that it does not examine the individual personal characteristics of mediators to determine why one mediator chooses strategy X when faced with a particular challenge while another mediator chooses strategy Y. We found more similarities than differences in choice of strategies by our mediators, but there is no denying that individual personality, level of experience, the type of case, and intuition must factor into these decisions. While the choice of particular strategies may become intuitive eventually, this text helps to shorten the learning curve for new mediators while adding a few new ideas for experienced mediators as they endeavor to select the most appropriate tool for addressing the challenges arising within their mediations.

Appendix

MEDIATOR BIOGRAPHIES

This list of mediator biographies provides insight into the type of experience and diversity within our panel of expert mediators participating in the benchmarking process, but is not an exhaustive list of participants. Some mediators chose to remain anonymous.

Sandi Adams, MSCM, has been working in the field of conflict resolution since 1982. She has provided training to many in the field and continues to offer direct mediation, facilitation, conflict coaching, and conflict resolution services. She is an ADR Advisor for Federal Emergency Management Agency (FEMA) and is on the roster for mediating Americans with Disabilities Act (ADA) complaint cases. She was director of the Mediation Training Program at Woodbury College in Montpelier, VT, principal staff at Friends Conflict Resolution Services in Philadelphia, PA, and taught at the University of North Carolina-Wilmington. She has her Masters of Science in Conflict Management from George Mason University. Author of *What the Fly Heard: What mediators say behind closed doors*, she was an associate editor of *Peacemaking in Your Neighborhood: Mediator's Handbook (Second Edition)*, and has published articles in various journals and magazines.
Sandi Adams shared her opinion and expertise in an online survey/focus group on March 4, 2011.

Evan A. Ash, Jr. has been a domestic mediator in Kansas's Tenth Judicial District since 1995, and serves as the supervisor for its clinical mediation programs. He began mediation as a chaplain and continued with the Neighborhood Justice Center of Wichita, Kansas. He taught mediation courses at

Johnson County Community College and Missouri Western State University, made numerous conference presentations and written articles for *Mediate.com* and the *Family Mediation News*. He is certified as an Advanced Practitioner of the Association for Conflict Resolution and served on the Family Section Advisory Council. He is a past President of the Heartland Mediators Association and a member of the Standards/Ethics Sub-Committee of the Kansas Office of Judicial Administration Dispute Resolution Advisory Council. He holds master's degrees from Seabury-Western Theological Seminary and the University of Nebraska.
Evan A. Ash Jr. shared his opinion and expertise in an online survey/focus group on March 3 and March 5, 2011.

Julie Barnes began mediating during her third year of law school. She was attracted to the alternative dispute resolution externship at the Fulton County Landlord/Tenant Court partly because of her educational background in Psychology and her work experience before law school, in social services. Julie Barnes is a registered neutral with the Georgia Office of Dispute Resolution. Since 2003, she has mediated hundreds of cases.
Julie Barnes shared her opinion and expertise in an online survey/focus group on March 2, 2011.

Vivian Berger, Esq. is the Nash Professor of Law Emerita at Columbia Law School. She has conducted hundreds of mediations since the mid-1990s and been designated an Advanced Practitioner in employment mediation—her specialty—by the Association for Conflict Resolution. She is a member of the American Arbitration Association Panel on Employment Mediation. She has also done arbitrations and independent workplace investigations and served as special master in a sexual harassment case in federal court. Professor Berger is on the mediator panels of the U.S. District Courts for the Southern and Eastern Districts of NY and the NJ state court system, for which she handles employment disputes. She also mediates for the U.S. Equal Employment Opportunity Commission (EEOC) and has mediated for the United States Postal Service (USPS) and the NY State Division of Human Rights. She publishes and speaks on mediation and employment-related topics.
Vivian Berger shared her opinion and expertise in an online survey/focus group on March 3 and November 6, 2011.

Edward Blumstein, JD, has been practicing law since 1959 and is a recognized practitioner and advocate of ADR. He has been a recognized family mediator since 1982. He is an Advanced Practitioner Member of the Association for Conflict Resolution. He served as an adjunct instructor of law at Temple University's Beasley School of Law from 1994 to 2006, where he

taught a clinical program in custody mediation—the nation's first such program. He received the 2006 Pennsylvania Bar Association's prestigious Sir Francis Bacon Award for Mediation Excellence and Advocacy. He is one of a dozen lawyer/mediators state-wide who are designated to mediate disputes within and between law firms for the Pennsylvania Bar Association's Lawyer Dispute Program. He mediates employment disputes for the U.S. Postal Service, the Transportation Security Administration, the National Archives, and U.S. Equal Employment Opportunity Commission (EEOC).
Edward Blumstein shared his opinion and expertise in an online survey/focus group on March 8, 2011.

Israela Adah Brill-Cass is executive director and ADR program manager at Boston Law Collaborative, LLC. In addition to her experience as a lawyer in private practice, she is also a skilled facilitator and trained mediator. Israela is a member of the Administrative Office of the Trial Court's Standing Committee on Dispute Resolution and she was Co-Chair of Massachusetts Continuing Legal Education (MCLE)'s First and Second Annual ADR and the Law Conferences (2009, 2010). She is part of MCLE's faculty for mediation training programs and has trained mediators for the American Bar Association. Israela designed and managed the Gillette/Procter and Gamble Severance Denial Appeal Program and she has designed and managed conflict resolution programs for the Superior Court and Commonwealth agencies. She created the first federally-funded Agricultural Mediation Program in New England. Israela develops and provides training for mediation, arbitration, negotiation and facilitation skills and she served on a national team of ADR professionals to develop technology quantifying the benefits of mediation.
Israela Adah Brill-Cass shared her opinion and expertise in an online survey/focus group on March 25 and November 7, 2011.

Chris Carlsten is a civil and domestic mediator in Georgia with special training for cases involving domestic violence. Ms. Carlsten has been a pioneer in the field of mediation in Georgia's courts and active with the Georgia Mediator's Association. She directed a conflict resolution program for the Fulton County Sheriff's Department for five years and taught mediation and conflict resolution at Emory, Georgia State University, and at the Fanning Institute at the University of Georgia.
Chris Carlsten shared her opinion and expertise in an online survey/focus group on March 12, 2011.

Lorig Charkoudian, PhD, is the executive director of the Community Mediation Maryland. Her work includes developing partnerships with state agencies including the Department of Public Safety and Correctional Service,

Maryland State Department of Education, Family Court Administration, and others, to bring collaborative conflict resolution to new and unique forums. Lorig serves as a trainer and provides technical assistance to the seventeen community based mediation programs serving Maryland. Lorig's research examines the impact of specific aspects of the mediation process on experiences for participants as well as broader cost-benefit analysis of community mediation. Community Mediation Maryland and Lorig have received national attention for the innovative work on prisoner reentry mediation.
Lorig Charkoudian shared her opinion and expertise in an online survey/focus group on March 7, 2011.

Jerome A. Diekemper, a licensed attorney in the State of Missouri since 1972, now focuses his work on alternative dispute resolution, especially mediation and arbitration. He has been selected by parties in over 1,200 disputes to serve as mediator. Jerome has been included in the first and every subsequent edition of the Best Lawyers in America. In the 2010 edition, he was listed in the areas of Alternative Dispute Resolution and Labor and Employment Law. He is a Fellow in the College of Labor and Employment Lawyers and an Advanced Workplace Practitioner in the Association of Conflict Resolution. He is also on the Mediation Panel and Labor Mediation Panel of the American Arbitration Association.
Jerome A. Diekemper shared his opinion and expertise in an online survey/focus group on March 2, March 22, April 1, and November 21, 2011.

Pamela Donison is the founder of Donison Law Firm, PLLC, a boutique family law firm in Phoenix, Arizona. Her practice specializes in family law and litigates, negotiates, mediates, and settles hundreds of family law cases, ranging from premarital agreements to post-decree custody issues. Pamela's practice is concentrated on Alternative Dispute Resolution (ADR), including arbitration, mediation, negotiation, and Collaborative Divorce. She is on the Maricopa County Superior Court Roster as an approved Attorney Mediator and Parenting Coordinator, and is a Judge Pro Tempore for the Family Bench. Pamela founded Arizona Collaborative Colleagues, a Phoenix-based practice group, was on the International Academy of Collaborative Professionals Institute Training Team (2011), and teaches both mediation and collaborative law. She frequently presents on family law issues as a guest lecturer at Arizona State University and Phoenix School of Law.
Pamela Donison shared her opinion and expertise in an online survey/focus group on November 7, 2011.

Dan Dozier is a partner in Press, Potter & Dozier, LLC where his practice is focused on providing the full range of ADR services. He has mediated hundreds of complex multiparty environmental, public policy, civil litigation,

and land use cases. Dozier was an adjunct professor at the Vermont Law School where he taught Environmental Dispute Resolution from 1989 to 2000. He has been admitted to the practice of law in Michigan, the District of Columbia, and Maryland.
Dan Dozier shared his opinion and expertise in an online survey/focus group on March 2, 2011.

Susan V. Edwards earned her law degree in 1979 from Villanova University on the Main Line in southeastern Pennsylvania. She earned her BA in sociology from Beaver College in 1969. She has additional education in family law, psychology, and mediation. Ms. Edwards is the Chair of the Family Section of the Association for Conflict Resolution. She is a charter member of MediationWorks, an organization that certifies mediators associated with the Chester County Pennsylvania Court of Common Pleas custody mediation program.
Susan V. Edwards shared her opinion and expertise in an online survey/focus group on March 14, April 10, and November 10, 2011.

Karena Ellis-Greenway is a member of the Royal Institution of Chartered Surveyors accredited mediator and a panel member of The Dispute Mediation Consultancy in the United Kingdom. She specializes in family mediation as well residential and commercial cases in which she provides surveys, valuation advice, expert witness reports and mediation in boundary/neighbor disputes. Karena holds a Urban Estates Management degree from Westminster University and was elected a professional member of the Royal Institution of Chartered Surveyors in 1996.
Karena Ellis-Greenway shared her opinion and expertise in an online survey/focus group on November 10th, 2011.

Bruce Engelbert is a former Federal employee with thirty-two years of service at the U.S. Environmental Protection Agency (EPA), the Department of Energy and the President's Council on Environmental Quality. His work focuses on promoting good public participation, customer service, and alternative dispute resolution. He is a certified mentor mediator in the State of Virginia and has mediated over 150 community, consumer, and employment cases. Mr. Engelbert has been an instructor at the Institute for Conflict Analysis and Resolution at Georgia Mason University and has taught facilitation and conflict resolution courses for corporate and government clients.
Bruce Engelbert shared his opinion and expertise in an online survey/focus group on March 4 and March 9, 2011.

Rachel Fishman Green, Esq. founded ReSolutions in 1995, a divorce and family mediation in Brooklyn. She was a member of the Board of Directors

of the Family & Divorce Mediation Council of Greater New York and was Chair of the Ethics Committee and the Domestic Violence Task Force. She was the Editor-in-Chief of their newsletter for five years. She presents frequently at conferences and seminars given by the NY State Council on Divorce Mediation and the Family & Divorce Mediation Council of Greater NY. She was the keynote speaker in 2002, at the annual conference for the Michigan Association of Court Mediators. She was awarded the achievement of the Advanced Practitioner Level Membership in the Academy of Family Mediators, the Association for Conflict Resolution, and is accredited by the NY State Council on Divorce Mediation.
Rachel Fishman Green shared her opinion and expertise in an online survey/focus group on March 2 and March 23, 2011.

John Ford is a mediator, trainer, and consultant. He teaches negotiation at University of California Hastings College of the Law, mediation at Golden Gate University, and is the trainer of the Northern California Human Resources Association's Mastering Mediation seminar.
John Ford shared his opinion and expertise in an online survey/focus group on March 2 and November 7, 2011.

Georgia Geiger has been a registered mediator in the State of Georgia since 1993. She has mediated cases in Superior Court, Juvenile Court, Probate Court, and Magistrate Court. Additionally, she has mediated in the field of special education and charter schools with the Georgia Department of Education. She is an Advanced Practitioner Member of the Family Section of the Association for Conflict Resolution. Georgia is a Licensed Professional Counselor and a National Board Certified Counselor. She is also in private practice in Counseling and Mediation.
Georgia Geiger shared her opinion and expertise in an online survey/focus group on March 7, 2011.

Steven J. Gold, Esq. has been a practicing attorney in Georgia since 1984, and has been practicing ADR since 1998. He has conducted over 1,500 ADR cases in personal injury, general civil, domestic relations through court-annexed programs and private sessions. He is registered with the Georgia Office of Dispute Resolution in General Mediation, Domestic Relations Mediation (including domestic violence), Arbitration, and Early Neutral Evaluation. Gold received his BA from Antioch College in 1973, and his JD from Emory University School of Law in 1983.
Steven J. Gold shared his opinion and expertise in an online survey/focus group on November 9, 2011.

Ericka Gray, DisputEd, has been a professional mediator, conflict resolution educator, and trainer since 1985. She has provided training throughout the world to thousands of mediators who mediate commercial, divorce and family, workplace, and community issues. She was Senior Mediator for JAMS' Boston Office and directed two Multi-Door Courthouses in New Jersey and Cambridge, MA. Ericka is on the faculty of Boston College Law School, Suffolk University Law School in Boston, MA and Northwestern University in Chicago. Ericka served on the Massachusetts Trial Court Standing Committee on Dispute Resolution and has been active in legislative activities related to dispute resolution. She holds Advanced Practitioner Member status in both the Family and the Workplace Sections of the Association for Conflict Resolution. She is a licensed psychologist.
Ericka Gray shared her opinion and expertise in an online survey/focus group on March 2nd, March 25 and November 7, 2011.

Don Greenstein, Esq. received a JD in law from Antioch School of Law in Washington, DC and has a background in law, negotiation, and dispute resolution and conflict management. With over twenty-eight years of experience in a broad array of technical issues, he excels at working with people in interpersonal conflict. Trained as a critical incident stress manager, Don is a Federal Emergency Management Agency (FEMA) Ombud/CADRE member. Don has over fifteen years of federal service engaged as an ADR attorney with the Department of Justice, United States Postal Service (USPS), U.S. Department of Defense, U.S. Navy, U.S. Air Force, U.S. Environmental Protection Agengy (EPA), U.S. Department of Transportation, Federal Emergency Management Agency (FEMA), and Department of Homeland Security (DHS).
Don Greenstein shared his opinion and expertise in an online survey/focus group on March 2 and March 23, 2011.

Alan Gross has mediated, arbitrated, facilitated, and trained at many venues in the North East USA, where he is currently serving as the Special Projects Coordinator for the New York Peace Institute. He has previously acted as Senior Director for Safe Horizon Mediation, ombudsman for the American Psychological Association, as an arbitrator for American Arbitration Association (AAA), Financial Industry Regulatory Authority (FINRA), and as a mediator for the Post Office and the U.S. Army. Gross was formerly Psychology Chair at the University of Maryland, a Fellow of the Association for Psychological Science, and the author of a textbook and more than fifty chapters and articles related to conflict resolution and social psychology. He is a Founding Member and Board Director of Mediators Beyond Borders.
Alan Gross shared his opinion and expertise in an online survey/focus group on November 8, 2011.

Daniel E. Gulden has mediated well over one thousand cases since 1990 for private parties, the American Arbitration Association (AAA), Financial Industry Regulatory Authority (FINRA), Georgia court systems, federal government agencies, and private organizations and currently serves as a full-time neutral. Approximately 75 percent of his practice involves mediation in business, commercial, employment, family, estate, small construction, personal injury, and securities; he also arbitrates in a number of these areas and trains and mentors other neutrals. As an attorney for over thirty years, Gulden has handled business, employment, tax, regulatory compliance, and estate issues, including as in-house counsel and chief administrative officer for a manufacturing company. He has a law degree from Emory University and an LLM from Georgetown University.
Daniel E. Gulden shared his opinion and expertise in an online survey/focus group on March 2 and November 19, 2011.

Timothy Hedeen, PhD, is a professor of conflict management at Kennesaw State University. He provides mediation services through court and private programs, delivers trainings in the areas of conflict resolution and communication, facilitates group and public policy decision making and planning, and conducts research and evaluation on dispute resolution and justice policy. He serves on the editorial boards of *Conflict Resolution Quarterly* and *Family Court Review*, as associate liaison to the Section Council of the American Bar Association Section of Dispute Resolution, and is a past chair of the Board of Directors of the National Association for Community Mediation. He is a senior consultant to the Consortium for Appropriate Dispute Resolution in Special Education, and research director of a U.S. national study of the collateral consequences of criminal convictions for the American Bar Association's Criminal Justice Section.
Timothy Hedeen shared his opinion and expertise in an online survey/focus group on November 5 and November 7, 2011.

Mary Kelleher-Forsyth has been a certified mediator in New York State (Unified Court System) for over fourteen years. She has conducted hundreds of mediations, facilitations, and trainings during this time. She has worked in the areas of criminal and civil suits and prosecutions, custody and visitation, parenting plans, student and student conflicts and special education. She has designed and conducted numerous Conflict Resolution and Peer Mediation programs for professionals and at risk student populations. She also presents regularly on the topic of Special Education Mediation and is an advocate for special education students and their families. She was one of the first graduates of the Columbia University Certificate program in Conflict Resolution and has a BA From Fordham University.

Mary Kelleher-Forsyth shared her opinion and expertise in an online survey/focus group on November 9, 2011.

Henry W. Kimmel has been a licensed attorney and registered mediator in Georgia since 1999. He has helped settle more than two thousand domestic, real estate, personal injury, contract and intellectual property issues. Before becoming a lawyer, he had extensive experience as a journalist, tennis professional, and real estate manager.
Henry W. Kimmel shared his opinion and expertise in an online survey/focus group on November 7, 2011.

Robert Leitch, a mediator and arbitrator since 1990, has served as a neutral in more than three thousand cases in many areas including commercial, divorce, non-compete/non-solicitation disputes, U.S. Olympic Committee-Olympic athletic competition, personal injury, real estate, securities, and sexual harassment. He taught alternative dispute resolution for Georgia State University Law School for seventeen years. He provided training of mediators and arbitrators over twenty-five times in seven states. He is a judge for the DeKalb County Magistrate and Decatur Municipal courts in Georgia. A graduate of Emory University's School of Law he also attended the London School of Economics and Political Science.
Robert Leitch shared his opinion and expertise in an online survey/focus group on March 12 and November 7, 2011.

David Lichter mediates and arbitrates cases throughout the United States and in Puerto Rico. He focuses on complex business litigation, securities, intellectual property, and bankruptcy matters. He has mediated and arbitrated approximately 1,250 cases and served as a special master and a special investigator in state and federal court. David is certified by the Florida Supreme Court as a Certified Civil Circuit and County Court mediator, and by the United States District Courts for the Southern and Middle Districts of Florida as a Certified Mediator and is listed in the Register of Mediators for the United States Bankruptcy Court for the Southern District of Florida. He is also a member of the Commercial Panel of Arbitrators and is a mediator for the American Arbitration Association and is an approved mediator for the Financial Industry Regulatory Authority.
David Lichter shared his opinion and expertise in an online survey/focus group on March 11 and November 7, 2011.

Frank A. Lightmas Jr. has been an Atlanta, Georgia, mediator, arbitrator, trial lawyer and commercial and business litigator for over thirty-five years. Frank is registered with the Georgia Office of Dispute Resolution as a neutral in the areas of arbitration, general mediation, and early neutral evaluation. He

has mediated several hundred cases, over 85 percent of which have been settled. A number have been complex, multiparty disputes involving hundreds of parties. He has also served as an arbitrator for over twenty-five years. Frank is a member of a several local Georgia judicial circuit panels of neutrals as well as many national and international panels such as the Financial Industry Regulatory Authority (FINRA), the International Institute for Conflict Prevention & Resolution (CPR), the Chartered Institute of Arbitrators (CIArb), the National Futures Association (NFA), the Georgia Academy of Mediators & Arbitrators, the National Academy of Distinguished Neutrals, and the International Mediation Institute.
Frank A. Lightmas, Jr. shared his opinion and expertise in an online survey/focus group on March 11 and November 7, 2011.

Sally Lord is an experienced Australian mediator specializing in Family Dispute Resolution at the Legal Aid Commission in New South Wales with an interest in cultural awareness and competence in mediation. She is a member of Mediators Beyond Borders and has an interest in online dispute resolution.
Sally Lord shared her opinion and expertise in an online survey/focus group on March 2 and March 23, 2011.

Robert J. McDonnell, MA APM has been providing mediation and dispute resolution services in New Jersey as principal of Alliance Mediation Services. An Accredited Professional Mediator (APM), Robert is approved by the New Jersey Administrative Office of the Courts (AOC) for the Statewide Mediation Program for Civil, General Equity, and Probate Cases and mediates civil matters for the AOC throughout Northern New Jersey. Robert also provides divorce mediation services, helping divorcing couples use mediation as an alternative to a contentious litigation. He was President of the New Jersey Association of Professional Mediators from 2008 to 2010 and currently serves on the Board of Directors as Immediate Past President.
Robert J. McDonnell shared his opinion and expertise in an online survey/focus group on March 12, 2011.

Robert Martell is Royal Institution of Chartered Surveyors Accredited Mediator in the United Kingdom and uses his communication skills gained over thirty years in the construction industry to facilitate and mediate agreements between parties.
Robert Martell shared his opinion and expertise in an online survey/focus group on November 7, 2011.

Andy G. Miller has been a full-time mediator for over seventeen years and more than one thousand cases. He mediates primarily employment and work-

place matters, but also has substantial experience mediating business, commercial, community, and church matters. He has mediated in fourteen states. Now in private practice, Mr. Miller was previously Director of Training Services for the Center for Conflict Resolution in Chicago for eight years. In addition, he has mediated cases for the state and federal courts and on a contract basis for other federal, state, and municipal agencies, including the U.S. Forest Service, the Charlotte, Indianapolis, and Chicago districts of the United States, U.S. Equal Employment Opportunity Commission (EEOC), the United States Postal Service, the Illinois Department of Human Rights, and the City of Chicago.
Andy G. Miller shared his opinion and expertise in an online survey/focus group on March 2 and November 7, 2011.

Tony Newport is a nationally accredited and leader accredited mediator. He focuses exclusively on workplace mediation and also runs conflict management, mediation, negotiation and communication training workshops in workplaces. He is a past co-chairman of the National Mediation Conference. He has presented papers on mediation in the workplace at the 2002, 2004, and 2010 NMC conferences in Canberra, Darwin, and Adelaide and at the Leader 2007 and 2009 international conferences in Wellington, NZ and Melbourne.
Tony Newport shared his opinion and expertise in an online survey/focus group on March 7 and March 22, 2011.

Douglas E. Noll, Esq. is a nationally acclaimed speaker, is also a full time mediator, specializing in difficult, complex, and intractable conflicts. He is a Fellow of the International Academy of Mediators, a Fellow of the American College of Civil Trial Mediators, on the American Arbitration Association panel of mediators and arbitrators, and is certified under international standards established by the International Mediation Institute. He is the author of *Elusive Peace: How Modern Diplomatic Strategies Could Better Resolve World Conflicts* (Prometheus, 2011) *Sex, Politics & Religion at the Office: The New Competitive Advantage* (Auberry Press 2006), with John Boogaert, and *Peacemaking: Practicing at the Intersection of Law and Human Conflict* (Cascadia 2002). Mr. Noll has been listed as one of the Best Lawyers in America since 2005 by US News & World Report, is a Northern California Super Lawyer and is one of 193 mediators selected for inclusion in the International Who's Who of Commercial Mediators.
Douglas E. Noll shared his opinion and expertise in an online survey/focus group on March 11, March 23, and November 7, 2011.

Julie K. Pinkus is a registered domestic mediator and registered civil mediator. A graduate of the Indiana University School of Law-Indianapolis, she

was a full-time magistrate in the Marion County Superior Court, Juvenile Division from 1990 to 1995 and has worked in private practice prior to completing the Domestic Relations Mediator training in January, 1997. She has mediated in excess of 1,500 cases and currently works exclusively as a mediator. Ms. Pinkus has been a speaker for Indiana Continuing Legal Education Forum (ICLEF) and NBI on various topics of mediation and family law. She is married to an attorney and is the mother of two teenagers.
Julie K. Pinkus shared her opinion and expertise in an online survey/focus group on November 7, 2011.

Greg Rooney has practiced mediation in Australia since 1991. He has mediated more than 1,500 disputes in a diverse range of conflicts including multi-party disputes involving government institutions, commercial and industrial disputes, agricultural disputes, franchise disputes, matrimonial disputes, and disputes involving conflict in the workplace. For the last eight years Rooney has mediated over 250 face-to-face mediations between religious leaders and individual victims of sexual abuse in the Catholic, Anglican, and Protestants religions in Australia. He has lectured in mediation, dispute system design, and Project Alliancing in a number of Australian universities, including the University of Queensland and Southern Cross University. Greg has conducted dispute resolution training for a number of public and private Australian institutions. He has published papers on mediating sexual abuse cases, the use of intuition in mediation, and Project Alliancing.
Greg Rooney shared his opinion and expertise in an online survey/focus group on March 22, 2011.

John E. Sands has arbitrated and mediated over four thousand employment law and labor-management disputes involving a wide range of issues. A graduate of Princeton and Yale Law School, Mr. Sands has chaired the Labor and Employment Law Sections of three bar associations, is vice president and a governor of the College of Labor and Employment Lawyers, and is a Fellow of the American College of Employee Benefit Counsel. Prior to becoming a full-time arbitrator and mediator, Mr. Sands was professor of law at the Albany Law School, general counsel of a government agency, and partner of a law firm representing employees, unions, and employee benefit funds. Mr. Sands is a widely-published author, and has lectured throughout the United States and Canada. His biographical entries have included *Who's Who in America*, in *American Law* and *Best Lawyers in America*.
John E. Sands shared his opinion and expertise in an online survey/focus group on March 11 and March 26, 2011.

Madeleine Sauvé spent the majority of her adult professional life as a mediator in the workplace context both in private practice for public and private

sector and First Nations clients, and in the role of mediator for various federal government departments. Her graduate research work centred on social conflict in the transition to First Nations self-government. Ms. Sauvé enjoyed the privilege of designing and delivering culturally informed training for Tlingit peacemakers in mediation. She is currently living on Cape Breton Island in the joyous capacity of shepherd and farmer.
Madeleine Sauvé shared her opinion and expertise in an online survey/focus group on March 9, 2011.

John Settle is an Association for Conflict Resolution advanced workplace mediator and Virginia Supreme Court—certified mediator. His is a member of the Virginia Bar, past President of the Virginia Mediation Network, and a former co-chair of the Workplace Section of Association for Conflict Resolution. His *Tips and Techniques: For Helping Parties Move Ahead and Overcome Roadblocks* is used for training by many mediation programs and schools. Although he began practice as a family mediator, he currently specializes in workplace mediation and training in conflict management.
John Settle shared his opinion and expertise in an online survey/focus group on March 2 and November 8, 2011.

G. Michael Smith has been a member of the Georgia Bar since 1975. Mr. Smith is engaged in business and corporate legal matters and personal injury work. He is versed in plaintiff and defense personal injury matters. In his business and corporate work he has acted as a general counsel for a publically traded chemical/pharmaceutical company. He works with companies which own intellectual properties and assists in contracting the licensing of the IP. He has hands-on experience in business transactions and has traveled to many countries to negotiate transactions for his clients. He is a member of American Arbitration Association (AAA) Commercial and Lemon Law Panels. He has mediated over 1900 cases. Smith has written and presented mediation papers at various CLE symposiums. Mr. Smith mediates with Miles Mediation and Arbitration services in Atlanta. He is a member of the Georgia Academy of Mediators and Arbitrators & the National Academy of Distinguished Neutrals.
G. Michael Smith shared his opinion and expertise in an online survey/focus group on March 2, 2011.

Doug Thompson is a senior mediator with the Keystone Center. Areas of special interest and expertise include enforcement case negotiation; conflicts concerning regulatory or policy matters; freshwater and marine issues and habitat protection disputes. Prior to The Keystone Center, he spent over twenty-five years with the U.S. Environmental Protection Agency (EPA) in various technical and management capacities including chief of wetland pro-

tection and chief of water enforcement. As part of EPA's dispute resolution program, he served as a mediator and facilitator for a number of environmental issues; he also worked on assignment at the U.S. Institute for Environmental Conflict Resolution in Tucson, Arizona. He has mediated extensively in the Massachusetts court system, is an adjunct faculty member of the University of Massachusetts Graduate Program in Dispute Resolution, and is a mediator and trainer with Metropolitan Mediation Services in Brookline, MA. He received a bachelor's degree in environmental science and a master's degree in biology from Northwestern University in Evanston, Illinois.
Doug Thompson shared his opinion and expertise in an online survey/focus group on March 25 and November 16, 2011.

Maartje Van-der-Vlies is an internationally recognized criminologist and mediator. She has worked for several Governments and the United Nations. As the author of many research projects into criminology she has appeared before dozens of Parliamentary Committees and contributed to serious changes in Criminal and Family Law.
Maartje Van-der-Vlies shared her opinion and expertise in an online survey/focus group on March 2, 2011.

Barbara Wilson, PhD, has been a family mediator since 1990, and is an independent practitioner and professional practice consultant. She is based in Portsmouth, Hampshire in the United Kingdom. Barbara is Accredited by the Family Mediators Association, recognized by the Legal Services Commission, and has extensive experience of mediating complex family and other disputes. She also led an independent adoption support agency. She has lectured on various postgraduate conflict resolution and mediation studies courses run jointly by the Institute of Family Therapy with the University of London. Barbara runs advanced workshops for mediators, and also trains other professionals in negotiation and conflict management strategies. Barbara is published in the UK and internationally.
Barbara Wilson shared her opinion and expertise in an online survey/focus group on November 8, 2011.

Jerry Wood currently serves as the director of the Fulton County Courts ADR Program in Georgia. He served as Chief Magistrate of Floyd County from 1997 to 2004, where he designed and implemented the county's first court connected mediation program. He received his BA from Shorter College in 1973, JD from Stetson University College of Law in 1978. He received the Master of Judicial Studies from the University of Nevada, Reno in 2010. Jerry is a member of the State Bar of Georgia, has published several articles on mediation, and has conducted numerous training events approved

for continuing education credits by the Georgia Office of Dispute Resolution and the State Bar of Georgia.
Jerry Wood shared his opinion and expertise in an online survey/focus group on March 15, March 22, March 23, and November 7, 2011.

Alex Yaroslavsky, is a mediator, arbitrator, and trainer with over seventeen years of conflict resolution experience. He is the founder of Yaro Group, LLC—a dispute resolution consultancy specializing in workplace conflict resolution. He is a member of several arbitration and mediation panels, including Financial Industry Regulatory Agency (FINRA), NY State Supreme Court Commercial Division, NYC Civilian Complaint Review Board, NY County Lawyers' Association, NJ Civil Court, and the US Bankruptcy Court (Eastern District). In addition to his consulting practice, Alex teaches several dispute resolution courses and is a board member of the Association for Conflict Resolution of Greater NY. He is also a member of the International Mediation Institute and is one of the first mediators certified by the NY State Dispute Resolution Association.
Alex Yaroslavsky shared his opinion and expertise in an online survey/focus group on March 2, 2011.

Dr. Susan Zaidel is an American-educated clinical psychologist (PhD, 1970, University of California, Los Angeles (UCLA)) who has been living in Israel since 1970. She specialized in marriage and family therapy in Israel and has been a Certified Family and Couple Therapist since 1990. Susan is also a Certified Family Mediator and a Certified Supervisor of Family Mediators (certification by the Israel Family Therapy Association). Together with an attorney colleague, she trains mediators in general mediation and in divorce mediation. She has authored books about divorce mediation (in Hebrew) for mediators and the general public and has published several articles about divorce and mediation in professional journals in the United States and in Israel. Although most of her work in private practice is as a psychologist and couples' therapist, she has mediated hundreds of divorces since her initial training in 1986.
Susan Zaidel shared her opinion and expertise in an online survey/focus group on March 2, April 3, and November 10, 2011.

Mediators who chose to remain anonymous

A total of seventeen family and divorce mediators, thirteen discrimination, workplace, and employment mediators as well as nine interpersonal conflict mediators chose to remain anonymous, but shared their opinion and expertise in an online survey /focus group between March 3 and November 24, 2011.

Bibliography

ABA (1990). "Civil Justice An Agenda For The 1990s" Report of the American Bar Association National Conference on Access to Justice in the 1990s, New Orleans, Louisiana, 1989. American Bar Association, 321 N. Clark St., Chicago, Illinois, 60610.

Allred, K.G. (2000). "Anger and retaliation in conflict: The role of attribution," in Deutsch, M. and P. Coleman (Eds.), *The Handbook of Conflict Resolution: Theory and Practice,* Jossey-Bass Publishers, San Francisco, CA, pp. 236–255.

American Bar Association. "Section on Dispute Resolution Competition for Representing Clients in Mediation," available at: http://www.americanbar.org/groups/dispute_resolution/awards_competitions/law_student_national_representation_in_mediation_competition.html (accessed 19 July 2011).

Avruch, K. (Spring 2003), "Type I and Type II Errors in Culturally Sensitive Conflict Resolution Practice," in *Conflict Resolution Quarterly,* Vol. 20 No. 3, pp. 351–371.

Bannink, F.P. (2007), "Solution-Focused Mediation: The Future with a Difference," in *Conflict Resolution Quarterly,* Vol. 25 No. 2, pp. 163–183.

Baron, R.A. (1989), "Personality and organizational conflict: Type A behavior pattern and self-monitoring," in *Organization Behavior and Human Decision Processes,* Vol. 44 No. 28, pp. 1–297.

Barsky, A., Este, D. and Collins, D. (Spring 1996), "Cultural Competence in Family Mediation," in *Conflict Resolution Quarterly,* Vol. 13 No. 3, pp. 167–178.

Beer, J. and Stief, E. (1997), *The Mediator's Handbook,* 3rd edition, Friends Conflict Resolution Program, New Society Publishers, Gabriola Island (British Columbia), Canada, 176 pages.

Benjamin, R.D. (Spring 1998), "Negotiation and Evil: The Sources of Religious and Moral Resistance to the Settlement of Conflicts," in *Conflict Resolution Quarterly,* Vol. 15 No. 3, pp. 245–266.

Bennett, M.D. and Hughes, S. (2005), *The Art of Mediation,* 2nd edition, National Institute for Trial Advocacy Inc., Notre Dame, IN, 269 pages.

Bingham, L.B., Kim, K. and Raines, S. (2002), "Exploring the Role of Representation In Employment Mediation at the United States Postal Service (USPS)," in *Ohio State. Journal on Dispute Resolution,* Vol. 17, pp. 341–378.

Brown. L.M. and Gilligan, C. (1992), *Meeting at the crossroads: Women's psychology and girls' development,* Harvard University Press, Cambridge, MA, 272 pages.

Bunker, B.B. and Rubin, J.Z. (Eds.), (1995), *Conflict, Cooperation and Justice: Essays Inspired by the Work of Morton Deutsch,* Jossey-Bass Publishers, San Francisco, CA, 441 pages.

Bush, R.A.B. and Folger, J.P. (2005), *The Promise of Mediation: The Transformative Approach to Conflict,* John Wiley & Sons, San Francisco, CA, 304 pages.

Bush, R.A.B and Folger, J.P. (1994), *The Promise of Mediation: Responding to conflict through empowerment and recognition,* Jossey-Bass Publishers, San Francisco, CA, 320 pages.

Charkoudian, L., Ritis, C.D., Buck, R. and Wilson, C.L. (2009), "Mediation by any other name would smell as sweet—or would it? The struggle to define mediation and its various approaches," in *Conflict Resolution Quarterly,* Vol. 26 No. 3, pp. 293–316.

Charkoudian, L. and Wayne, E.K. (Fall 2010), "Fairness, Understanding, and Satisfaction: Impact of Mediator and Participant Race and Gender on Participants' Perception of Mediation," in *Conflict Resolution Quarterly,* Vol. 28 No. 1, pp. 23–52.

Cobb, S. and Rifkin, J. (1991), "Practice and Paradox: Deconstructing Neutrality in Mediation," in *Law & Social Inquiry,* Vol. 16 No. 1, pp. 35–62.

Cohen, O., Dattner, N. and Luxenburg, A. (Summer 1999), "The limits of the mediator's neutrality," in *Conflict Resolution Quarterly,* Vol. 16 No. 4, pp. 341–348.

Conley Tyler, M. and Raines, S.S. (Spring 2006), "Colloquy: The human face of on-line dispute resolution," in *Conflict Resolution Quarterly,* Vol. 23 No. 3, pp. 333–342.

Damelio, R. (1995), *The Basics of Benchmarking,* Productivity Press, Portland, OR, 80 pages.

Davidheiser, M. (Spring 2006), "Harmony, peacemaking, and power: Controlling processes and African mediation," in *Conflict Resolution Quarterly,* Vol. 23 No. 3, pp. 281–299.

Deutsch, M. and Coleman, P. (2001), *The Handbook of Conflict Resolution Theory and Practice,* Jossey-Bass Publishers, San Francisco, CA, 649 pages.

Druckman, D. and Olekalns, M. (2008), "Emotions in negotiation," in *Group Decisions & Negotiation,* Vol. 17 No. 1, pp. 1–11.

Faure, G.O. (Fall 2011), "Practice Note: Informal Mediation in China," in *Conflict Resolution Quarterly,* Vol. 29 No. 1, pp. 85–99.

Fisher, R. and Ury, W. (1981), *Getting to Yes: Negotiating Agreement Without Giving In,* Penguin Books, New York, NY, 200 pages.

Fisher, R. and Ury, W. (1991), *Getting to Yes: Negotiating Agreement Without Giving In,* Houghton Mifflin Company, New York, NY, 200 pages.

Folger, J.P., Poole, M.S. and Stutman, R.K. (2001), *Working Through Conflict: Strategies for Relationships, Groups and Organizations,* Longman, London, England, 356 pages.

Gerami, A. (2009), "Bridging the theory-and-practice gap: Mediator power in practice," in *Conflict Resolution Quarterly,* Vol. 26 No. 4, pp. 433–451.

Goldberg, R.M. (2009), "How our worldviews shape our practice," in *Conflict Resolution Quarterly,* Vol. 26 No. 4, pp. 405–431.

Goldberg, S.B., Sander, F.E.A., Rogers, N.H. and S.R. Cole, S.R. (2007), *Dispute Resolution: Negotiation, Mediation and Other Processes,* Wolters Klewer Law & Business Publishing, Chicago, IL, 790 pages.

Green, M.Z. (2003), "Finding lawyers for employees in discrimination disputes as a critical prescription for unions to embrace racial justice," in *University of Pennsylvania Journal of Labor and Employment Law,* Vol. 7 No. 1, pp. 55–118.

Gunnar, M.R. and Fisher, P.A. (2006), "Bringing basic research on early experience and stress neurobiology to bear on preventive interventions for neglected and maltreated children," in *Development and Psychopathology,* Vol. 18 No. 3, pp. 651–677.

Hairston, C.D. (Summer 1999), "African Americans in mediation literature: A neglected population," in *Conflict Resolution Quarterly,* Vol. 16 No. 4, pp. 357–375.

Hale, C. L. and Nix, C. (March 1997), "Achieving neutrality and impartiality: The ultimate communication challenge for peer mediators," in *Conflict Resolution Quarterly,* Vol. 14 No. 4, pp. 337–352.

Hanycz, C.M. (2005), "Civil Justice and Civil Justice Reform: Through the Looking Glass: Mediator Conceptions of Philosophy, Process and Power," in *Alberta Law Review,* Issue 42 (special issue), pp. 819–885.

Haslam, S.S. (2004), *Psychology in organizations: The social identity approach* (2nd edition), Sage Publications Ltd., Thousand Oaks, CA, 306 pages.

Haynes, J.M., Haynes, G.L. and Fong, L.S. (2004), *Mediation: Positive Conflict Management*, State University of New York, Albany, NY, 280 pages.

Hedeen, T. (Summer 2003), "Institutionalizing Community Mediation: Can Dispute Resolution of, by, and for the People Long Endure?," in *Penn State Law Review*, Vol. 108 No. 1, pp. 265–276.

Hedeen, T. and Coy, P.G. (2000), "Community Mediation and the Court System: The Ties That Bind," in *Mediation Quarterly*, Vol. 17 No. 4, pp. 351–367.

Howard, W.M. (Oct.–Dec. 1995), "Arbitrating Claims of Employment Discrimination: What Really Does Happen? What Really Should Happen?" in *Dispute Resolution Journal*, pp. 40–50.

Irvine, M. (February/April 2003), "Some do's and don'ts of mediation advocacy," in *Dispute Resolution Journal*, pp. 45–47.

Kelly, J.B. (Winter 1995), "Power imbalance in divorce and interpersonal mediation: Assessment and intervention," in *Conflict Resolution Quarterly*, Vol. 13 No. 2, pp. 85–98.

Levine-Finley, S. and Carter, J.S. (Winter 2010), "Then and now: Interviews with expert U.S. organizational ombudsmen," in *Conflict Resolution Quarterly*, Vol. 28 No. 2, pp. 111–139.

Lewicki, R.J. and Bunker, B.B. "Trust in Relationships: A Model of Development and Decline," in Bunker, B.B. and Rubin, J.Z. (Eds.), (1995), *Conflict, Cooperation and Justice: Essays Inspired by the Work of Morton Deutsch*, Jossey-Bass Publishers, San Francisco, CA, 441 pages.

Lewicki, R., Barry, B. and Saunders, D.M. (2009), *Negotiation (Sixth Edition)*. McGraw-Hill Education Series (USA), 640 pages.

Li-On, L. (Summer 2009), "The politics of community mediation: A study of community mediation in Israel," in *Conflict Resolution Quarterly*, Vol. 26 No. 4, pp. 453–479.

Markey, S. (September 17, 2003), "Monkeys show sense of fairness, study says," in *National Geographic News*, available at: http://news.nationalgeographic.com/news/2003/09/0917_030917_monkeyfairness.html (accessed 29 March 2011).

Maslow, A. H. (1943). "A theory of human motivation." in *Psychological Review*, No. 50, pp. 370–396.

Mayer, R.C., Davis, J.H. and Schoorman, D.F. (July 1995), "An Integrative Model of Organizational Trust," in *The Academy of Management Review*, Vol. 20 No. 3, pp. 709–734.

McEwen, C.A. and Maiman, R.J. (1984), "Mediation in Small Claims Court: Achieving Compliance Through Consent," in *Law and Society Review*, Vol. 18 No. 1, pp. 11–49.

Meyerson, B.E. (2009), "Preparing for Mediation: Effective Representation of Clients," available at: http://www.brucemeyerson.com/articles/a_001.html (accessed 1 October 2011).

Moore, C. (2003), *The mediation process: Practical strategies for resolving conflict* (3rd edition), Jossey-Bass Publishers, Sans Francisco, CA, 599 pages.

Morris, C. (1997), "The Trusted Mediator: Ethics and Interaction in Mediation," in Macfarlane, J. (Ed.), (1997), Rethinking Disputes: The Mediation Alternative, Cavendish Publishing Limited (London, UK) and Emond-Montgomery Publication Limited (Toronto, Canada), pp. 301–347.

Neuliep, J. (2009), *Intercultural Communication: A Contextual Approach*, (4th edition), Sage Publications, Thousand Oaks, CA, 496 pages.

Nielsen, L.B. and Beim, A. (2004), "Media Misrepresentation: Title VII, Print Media, and Public Perceptions of Discrimination Litigation," in *Stanford Law and Policy Review*, Vol. 15, p. 237.

Ogawa, N. (Fall 1999), "The Concept of Facework: Its Function in the Hawaii Model of Mediation," in *Conflict Resolution Quarterly*, Vol. 17 No. 1, pp. 5–20.

Pely, D. (Fall 2010) "Honor: The Sulha's Main Dispute Resolution Tool," in *Conflict Resolution Quarterly*, Vol. 28 No. 1, pp. 67–81.

Poitras, J. (July 2008), "What Makes Parties Trust Their Mediator?" in *Conflict Resolution Quarterly*, Vol. 22 No. 4, pp. 437–451.

Poitras, J, Stimec, A. and Roberge, J.F. (January 2010). "The Negative Impact of Attorneys on Mediation Outcomes: A Myth or Reality?" in *Negotiation Journal*, Vol. 26 No. 1, pp. 9-24.

Raines, S. and Kubala, D. (June 2011) "Environmental Conflict Resolution by Water Utilities: Applications and Lessons Learned," in *Journal of the American Water Works Association,* Vol. 103 No. 6, pp. 61–70.

Raines, S.S. (Summer 2005), "Can online mediation be transformative? Tales from the front," in *Conflict Resolution Quarterly,* Vol. 22 No. 4, pp. 437–451.

Rifkin, J., Millen, J. and Cobb, S. (Winter 1991), "Toward a new discourse for mediation: A critique of neutrality," in *Conflict Resolution Quarterly,* Vol. 9 No. 2, pp. 151–164.

Rosenbloom, J.D. (2002). "Exploring Methods to Improve Management and Fairness in Pro Se Cases: A Study of the Pro Se Docket in the Southern District of New York" in *Fordham Urban Law Journal*, Vol. 30 No. 1, pp. 305-399.

Ross, L. and Stillinger, C. (1991), "Barriers to conflict resolution," in *Negotiation Journal,* Vol. 7 No. 4, pp. 389–405.

Rubin, J.Z., Pruitt, D.G., and Kim, S.H. (1994), Social Conflict: Escalation, Stalemate, and Settlement (2nd edition), McGraw-Hill, New York, NY, 288 pages.

Spier, R.G. (September–October 1999), "Practice aids: The ten biggest mistakes lawyers make in mediation," in *Commercial Law Bulletin,* pp. 22–24.

Stapenhurst, T. (2009), *The Benchmarking Book: A How-To-Guide to Best Practice for Managers and Practitioners,* Butterworth-Heinemann, Boston, MA, 496 pages .

Stimec, A. and Poitras, J. (Spring 2009), "Building trust with parties: Are mediators overdoing it?" in *Conflict Resolution Quarterly*, Vol. 26 No. 3, pp. 317–331.

Tannen, D. (1990), *You Just Don't Understand: Women and Men in Conversation,* Oxford University Press, New York, NY, 352 pages.

Thomas, K.W. and Kilmann, R.H. (1974), *Thomas-Kilmann Conflict Modes Assessment Tool,* available at: http://www.kilmann.com/conflict.html (retrieved 25 April 2011).

Vedantam, S. (2007), "If it feels good to be good, it might be only natural," in *The Washington Post,* 28 May, available at: http://www.washingtonpost.com/wp-dyn/content/article/2007/05/27/AR2007052701056.html (accessed 23 April 2010).

Volkema, R.J. (Winter 1988), "The mediator as face manager," in *Conflict Resolution Quarterly,* Vol. 1988 No. 22, pp. 5–14.

Wall, J. A. and Chan-Serafin, S. (2009). "Processes in civil case mediations." in *Conflict Resolution Quarterly*, Vol. 26 No. 3, pp. 262–291.

Wall, J., Dunne, T. and Chan-Serafin, S. (Winter 2011), "The effects of neutral, evaluative, and pressing mediation strategies," in *Conflict Resolution Quarterly,* Vol. 29 No. 2, pp. 127–150.

Watson, C. (April 1994), "Gender versus power as a predictor of negotiation behaviors and outcomes," in *Negotiation Journal,* Vol. 10 No. 2, pp. 117–127.

Wilmot, W.W. and Hocker, J.L. (2000), *Interpersonal Conflict* (6th edition), McGraw-Hill Higher Education, New York, NY, 360 pages.

Wing, L. (Summer 2009), "Mediation and inequality reconsidered: Bringing the discussion to the table," in *Conflict Resolution Quarterly,* Vol. 26 No. 4, pp. 383–404.

Index

About the Authors

Jean Poitras is an associate professor of conflict management at HEC Montréal in Canada. He developed comprehensive knowledge of conflict management through his experience as a consultant and mediator as well as the findings of his studies. His research program focuses on the intervention strategies used in mediation and negotiation. Professor Poitras has published numerous articles and books on mediation, negotiationm and conflict management. He is a member of the editorial review boards of several scholarly journals: *Conflict Resolution Quarterly*, *International Journal of Conflict Management*, *Negotiation and Conflict Management Research*, *Negotiation Journal and Négociations*. Professor Poitras won the 2012 Outstanding Reviewer Award from the Emerald Literati Network. For more than fifteen years now, Jean Poitras has been helping professionals develop their negotiation and mediation skills.

Susan Raines is a professor of conflict management at Kennesaw State University (Georgia, USA). Professor Raines has designed and evaluated conflict management systems for the United States Postal Service, the U.S. Environmental Protection Agency, the Florida Supreme Court, the Indiana Department of Environmental Management, the DeKalb County (GA) Dispute Resolution Center, as well as for several private sector employers (many of whom require confidentiality as part of their contract). Additionally, she has mediated and arbitrated more than ten thousand commercial and civil disputes, trained commercial mediators and arbitrators for the European Union, trained United Nations managers in conflict management, intervened in many workplace conflicts for various consulates based in Atlanta and abroad, etc. She has published scholarly articles on mediation and best practices in mediation training and is also the editor of *Conflict Resolution Quarterly*.